There are few living pa
His writing always help
insights and seasoned pas....
is no exception. I wish this book had existed when I was younger;
I'm thrilled it exists now. Buy several copies and hand them out
liberally.

Matt Smethurst
Managing editor, The Gospel Coalition
Author of *Before You Open Your Bible: Nine Heart Postures for*
Approaching God's Word

It seems like the Church is to Christianity what silent letters are
to words. Everyone knows it is necessary, but very few people
know why. Garrett does the job of a good teacher—or maybe
even a good mechanic. He takes apart the pieces that make up
the Church (one by one), shows their importance and necessity
and puts them back together seamlessly. The end result is that
the reader is more than just convinced of the Church's necessity,
they become captivated by its beauty. Such a helpful resource for
everyone who finds themselves walking through the front doors
of any church.

John Onwuchekwa
Pastor, Cornerstone Church, Atlanta, Georgia

CHURCH

DO I HAVE TO GO?

J. GARRETT KELL
SERIES EDITED BY MEZ MCCONNELL

CHRISTIAN
FOCUS

Copyright © J. Garrett Kell 2019

paperback ISBN 978-1-5271-0426-6
epub ISBN 978-1-5271-0488-4
mobi ISBN 978-1-5271-0489-1

10 9 8 7 6 5 4 3 2 1

Published in 2019
Reprinted in 2020
by
Christian Focus Publications Ltd,
Geanies House, Fearn, Ross-shire,
IV20 1TW, Great Britain.

www.christianfocus.com

Cover and interior design by Rubner Durais

Printed in China

CONTENTS

PREFACE

The fact that I'm writing a book about the church seems a bit strange to me. I went to church as a child, but found it irrelevant. In high school and college, I sat in the church's balcony, usually hung over from partying the night before. To me, Jesus was no more real than Bigfoot or the Tooth Fairy. But God changed all of that near the end of my time in college. A friend shared about the forgiveness of Jesus during a party which began a complete transformation in my life. At first, I was isolated from other Christians, but quickly learned how much I need the church and the church needs me. Today I serve as a pastor of a congregation just outside Washington, DC. We are not a bunch of perfect people, but each week we gather around the grace of God in Christ Jesus. Together, we help each other to heaven by encouraging each other to resist sin and cling to the promises of God by faith. My prayer is that this brief book will help you to do the same, wherever God may have placed you.

J. Garrett Kell
May 2019

SERIES INTRODUCTION

The First Steps series will help equip those from an unchurched background take the first steps in following Jesus. We call this the 'pathway to service' as we believe that every Christian should be equipped to be of service to Christ and His church no matter your background or life experience.

If you are a church leader doing ministry in hard places, use these books as a tool to help grow those who are unfamiliar with the teachings of Jesus into new disciples. These books will equip them to grow in character, knowledge and action.

Or if you yourself are new to the Christian faith, still struggling to make sense of what a Christian is, or what the Bible actually says, then this is an easy to understand guide as you take your first steps as a follower of Jesus.

There are many ways to use these books.

+ They could be used by an individual who simply reads through the content and works through the questions on their own.

+ They could be used in a one-to-one setting, where two people read through the material before they meet and then discuss the questions together.

+ They could be used in a group setting where a leader presents the material as a talk, stopping for group discussion throughout.

Your setting will determine how you best use this resource.

A USER'S KEY:

As you work through the studies you will come across the following symbols…

BRIAN – I'm going to introduce you to Brian. There will be times in each chapter when you'll hear something about his story and what's been going on in his life. We want you to take what we've been learning from the Bible and think about what difference it would make in Brian's life and our own. So, whenever you see this symbol you'll hear a bit more about what's going on with him.

ILLUSTRATION – Through real-life examples and scenarios, these sections help us to understand the point that's being made.

STOP – When we hit an important or hard point we'll ask you to stop and spend some time thinking or chatting through what we've just learnt. This might be answering some questions, or it might be hearing more of Brian's story.

KEY VERSE – The Bible is God's Word to us, and therefore it is the final word to us on everything we are to believe and how we are to behave. Therefore we want to read the Bible first, and we want to read it carefully. So whenever you see this symbol you are to read or listen to the Bible passage three times. If the person you're reading the Bible with feels comfortable, get them to read it at least once.

MEMORY VERSE – At the end of each chapter we'll suggest a Bible verse for memorisation. We have found Bible memorisation to be really effective in our context. The verse (or verses) will be directly related to what we've covered in the chapter.

SUMMARY – Also, at the end of each chapter we've included a short summary of the content of that chapter. If you're working your way through the book with another person, this might be useful to revisit when picking up from a previous week.

MEET BRIAN

Brian grew up in a small town in the hills of West Virginia, USA. Home was a smoky, worn-down trailer that leaked when it rained. His father's drunken tantrums coupled with his mother's absence made it an unhappy place. Brian's dad often flirted with his girlfriends, but Brian was happy to fight him if necessary.

Life was hard for Brian, but he found ways to overcome. His friends knew him as the life of the party, until the summer day that changed him forever. He and a group of friends had gone fishing at a river. Near the end of the day, they decided to jump from a cliff. Brian's friends jumped, and they all made it back to shore, except one. His best friend Nathan disappeared under the muddy current and wasn't found until it was too late.

The next week was brutal. Tears dampened his pillow as anger, grief, and guilt haunted him. Answerless questions haunted his mind, and made life nearly unbearable. Brian wondered: Why did Nathan die? What happened to him when he died? Why didn't *he* die instead? What *if it had been* Brian who had drowned? Where would he go when *he* died?

At Nathan's funeral, a pastor spoke of a Saviour who came to give peace in the midst of our darkest days. Brian wanted that peace, but didn't know how to find it.

Thankfully, help came the following week. During an afternoon lull, a co-worker named James approached Brian and told him he'd been praying for him. Brian was usually annoyed by religious chitchat, but that day he felt thankful. As they talked, James explained that Jesus died and rose so that we could know God's peace. Later that night, Brian couldn't stop thinking about what he'd heard, and when he woke up the next morning, he decided to visit a church.

WHAT'S THE POINT?

The church is a people, not a place.

1. WHAT IS THE CHURCH?

 BRIAN

Brian sat in the parking lot for nearly twenty minutes. He'd already finished two cigarettes and a third twirled between his fingers. He watched people park their cars and enter the church, but felt increasingly sure he didn't belong. As he saw people walk in, smile, and wave to one another, Brian knew these people lacked the problems he couldn't escape.

Brian had always been wary about church. His grandmother had taken him a few times when he was young, but most of his knowledge came from what he'd seen on late-night TV.

Deep down, he knew church wasn't for him. But for some reason, he couldn't leave the parking lot. His newfound interest in Jesus urged him to stay. After a few drags on his cigarette, he pushed past his reasons to leave and took a seat near the back of the room.

STOP

What kinds of experiences have you had with church? What feelings did you have when you first visited one? Does Brian have any reason to think he could find help there?

 'I will build my church and the gates of hell will not prevail against it' – Jesus (Matt. 16:18).

The church is not what it seems.

Most people think of it as a building or an event—or, if they come from a charismatic background, they may think they 'had some church' when Aunt Betty got filled by the Holy Spirit and ran a few laps around the pews.

While some use the word 'church' this way, it isn't exactly correct. When Jesus says He will build His church, He's not talking about building a physical building like the one Brian walked into. He's talking about something much more amazing.

You see, the church is actually a people, not a place or thing.

The word 'church' means 'assembly.' It's an assembly or gathering of people who believe good news about Jesus. They believe Jesus takes people who are far from Him and makes them His very own people by His grace. That means that as Brian sat there, he was in a 'church' building during a 'church' service, but he was also with *the church, the people of God.*

 'Now in Christ Jesus you who once were far off have been brought near by the blood of Christ.' – (Eph. 2:13).

The Bible tells us that everyone starts on the wrong side of God. We begin as rebels against Him. We've not loved Him or obeyed His commands. Because God is good, He will judge us. He will allow no evil, small or great, to be overlooked in His universe.

And yet, despite how we've treated God, He has provided a way for us to be forgiven. God sent His Son Jesus to live a perfect life, die on a cross to take the judgment for sinners, and then rise from the dead in order to give new life. In other words,

Jesus took the death sentence *we* deserved for our sins

and not only forgives those who trust in Him,

but also brings them into His family as those loved by God.

Though Brian didn't realize it when he walked into the building that morning, he'd stepped into a room of people just like him. Sure, they may have come from different walks of life. On the outside, they probably looked different from him. But every person there had one major thing in common: they were all in desperate need of God's mercy.

This is what makes the church so amazing. I've heard it said that the church is not a museum of people who have it all together, but a hospital where broken people receive help from God and one another.

STOP

If the church is a gathering of people who have been rescued from their sin, what do you think would make those people unique? How do you think they should treat each other? What do you think they would talk about when they spend time together?

 ## ILLUSTRATION

I once lived in Texas. When I moved there, I expected to see a lot of cowboys and horses, which I did. But you know what I saw almost everywhere? The Texas flag. The star of Texas flew on flags, covered walls, and was even tattooed on bodies. Everywhere I went, I saw the red, blue, and white symbol that declared, 'You're in Texas.'

Full of people marked out as God's, churches should act similarly. They should show that they are His by being

worshipful,

holy,

and loving.

'Let us be grateful for receiving a kingdom that cannot be shaken, and thus let us offer to God acceptable worship, with reverence and awe, for our God is a consuming fire' (Heb. 12:28-29).

Everyone worships something. Before we become Christians, we look to things like money, sex, drugs, food, comfort, or fame to give us peace and joy. The Bible calls these idols because they take the place of God in our hearts and receive the devotion only He deserves.

The good news is that Jesus changes our hearts, which changes our worship.

The church has been rescued from worshipping false things,

and now we're devoted to worshipping God with reverence and joy.

Worship happens when the church gathers to pray, sing, hear, and obey God's Word. It also happens when churches observe the Lord's Supper and baptism. But worship is a way of life. Romans 12:1 says, *'I appeal to you therefore, brothers, by the mercies of God, to present your bodies as a living sacrifice, holy and acceptable to God, which is your spiritual worship.'*

The church is to be a people who worship God when they gather together, and when they scatter into the world.

STOP

What were the idols you used to worship before you began following Jesus? How do they still tempt you? What do you think it means to worship God rightly?

'As obedient children, do not be conformed to the passions of your former ignorance, but as he who called you is holy, you also be holy in

all your conduct, since it is written, "You shall be holy, for I am holy." (1 Pet. 1:14-16).

The church is a people called to be holy.

The word 'holy' means 'set apart.' The church is set apart from sin and set apart to God. This means a church's members used to love sin; they used to do whatever they wanted. But now, because God has rescued them, they live for Him. They fight against sin, they live for eternal things, and they do what pleases God. Of course Christians won't be perfect, but they will experience victory over sin.

> **STOP**
>
> *If the church is set apart from sin and set apart to God, how would that look in their everyday lives? How would it make them different than the world around them? How might that give hope to people like Brian who have felt like slaves to destructive habits?*

 'A new commandment I give to you, that you love one another: just as I have loved you, you also are to love one another. By this all people will know that you are my disciples, if you have love for one another.' – Jesus (John 13:34-35).

The church is a people marked by love.

They love God by obeying Him (John 14:15), and they love one another by imitating His love for them (1 John 4:11). Jesus showed great compassion, patience, and sacrifice in His love for the church. He was not selfish when He died on the cross. He was a servant who gave His life so that others could live.

STOP

What would it be like if the church always related to one another as Jesus related to them? How would that compare to the way people are treated in the world?

BRIAN

When Brian entered the building, he sat among people who were different from anything he'd ever encountered. They didn't seem like perfect people, but they did seem like people who were being changed. Brian didn't realize it yet, but as he sat with the church, he sat with people who would show him who God was in a way he never could have imagined.

Because the concept of church seems abstract, the Bible uses several word pictures to help us understand. As we investigate, we'll see that God says the church is like

a body,

a house,

a family,

and a bride.

ILLUSTRATION

It's incredible how the body works. Have you ever thought about it? Right now, your eyes are seeing these words while your hands hold the book. Your ears hear noises, and your feet are ready to take you wherever you need to go. Your body parts work together to help you do whatever you desire. That's incredible, isn't it?

The church is described in a similar way.

'Just as the body is one and has many members, and all the members of the body, though many, are one body, so it is with Christ' (1 Cor. 12:12).

God says the church is like a body.

Just as a healthy physical body has individual parts that work, so it is in the church. Each individual person is part of a whole, and each part is vitally important. God has designed the church to work in unison to fulfil His purposes in the world (Eph. 4:16). In a very real sense, the church is God's hands, feet, eyes, and mouth in a world that desperately needs to see what He is like.

STOP

If it's true that God has created us to contribute to fulfilling His plans, how does that change the way we think about our purpose in life? How does it change the way a church should work together?

 ILLUSTRATION

Family reunions are strange. Relatives gather together to meet, eat, and catch up on their lives. At family reunions you find people you know well, people whose names you forget, and people you love but are a little crazy.

The church is a little like a family reunion. When we gather as a church, we're all related—not by blood, but by the fact that through Jesus, we're a family of forgiven misfits united by God's Spirit.

As with any family, there can be difficult relationships, but God gives grace to help us learn to love one another.

'I will be a Father to you, and you shall be sons and daughters to Me, says the Lord Almighty' (2 Cor. 6:18).

When we repent of our sin and believe in Jesus, every relationship we have changes. God becomes our Father. Jesus becomes our older brother (Heb. 2:11-13). Other Christians become our brothers and sisters. Though our church family has issues, we're to be marked by love for one another (Heb. 13:1).

BRIAN

To say Brian's biological family was dysfunctional would be a compliment. But when he sat among the church, he sat among a family that was quite different. Sure, they had sin struggles that made relationships challenging, but Jesus was building this family together in love. Brian had good reason to be sceptical of these strangers, but in the church he would find a family that love would hold together.

STOP

What would it mean to you to know that you have a new family in Jesus? When you hear that God is your Father, what feelings does that stir up in you? How does it affect the way you relate to other church members when you know that God says you are their brother or sister?

ILLUSTRATION

My house is on a small street. The outside walls are made of brick, it has a fence that keeps our dogs from tearing up the neighbourhood and rooms filled with furniture. What makes the place special? My wife and children who live there with me. Their presence is what makes the place special.

God tells us in the Scriptures that believers in Jesus are the place in which His Spirit dwells. This means His people are very special to Him because He has chosen to live with them.

'You yourselves like living stones are being built up as a spiritual house, to be a holy priesthood, to offer spiritual sacrifices acceptable to God through Jesus Christ' (1 Pet. 2:5).

 'Do you not know that you [plural] are God's temple and that God's Spirit dwells in you? If anyone destroys God's temple, God will destroy him. For God's temple is holy, and you are that temple' (1 Cor. 3:16-17).

In the days before Jesus came, God chose to dwell in a house called a temple. He wasn't *limited* to that place (God is everywhere), but in a very real sense, He humbled Himself by dwelling in a temple made of stone.

He did this so that His people could be near to Him and enjoy His presence.

But when Jesus came, everything changed.

God now dwelt *among us* (John 1:14).

After Jesus rose from the dead, God the Father sent His Spirit to live in His people. Again, this means the church is *not* just a building, but a people who have God's Spirit living within them (Eph. 2:19-22).

STOP

What does it say about God that He chooses to live inside His people? How does this affect the way we think about Him as a personal God?

 ILLUSTRATION

In nearly every culture, the bride is celebrated. On her wedding day, she's dressed beautifully and made ready for her husband. His heart is full with hope and love. After their wedding, she's to be treated with honour and love while she faithfully loves her husband.

Though many marriages are bad pictures of what God intended, there's great beauty in God's gift of marriage. The love of a husband for his bride gives us a glimpse into the kind of love God has for His people. Similar to marriage, God

takes His people to Himself,

makes a covenant with them,

and promises to love them for the rest of their lives.

"'Therefore a man shall leave his father and mother and hold fast to his wife, and the two shall become one flesh.' This mystery is profound, and I am saying that it refers to Christ and the church' (Eph. 5:31-32).

'Come, I will show you the Bride, the wife of the Lamb' – An Angel of God (Rev. 21:9).

Though we're unfaithful to God through our sin, He has forgiven us and given us to Jesus as His beloved bride. Jesus is a faithful husband who loves His church with tender, compassionate care. This should move His church to love Him with faithfulness and purity (2 Cor. 11:2). It should also stir in us a great anticipation to see Him face to face, which is why we say with the rest of God's people, 'Come, Lord Jesus!' (Rev. 22:20).

Because the church is so unlike anything else in the world, God uses many illustrations to help us comprehend. He desires for us to come away with this stunning reality:

the church is a people loved by God.

For reasons beyond our wildest imagination, He chooses to have a relationship with His people and uses some of the most intimate metaphors possible to describe it.

STOP

Why do you think it matters that we see the church as a people rather than a place?

How does the image of the church as Jesus' bride encourage you?

What reasons could you come up with as to why God should not love you? How are you encouraged by the fact that He does?

If the church was really a bunch of messed up people who desired to follow God, would you want to be a part of it?

BRIAN

After the service, a grey-haired couple approached Brian. They introduced themselves as Dave and Ashley and began to ask him questions about where he was from and how he enjoyed the service. After the small talk, they invited him to have lunch at their home. Though he was a little unsure, he was thankful for their kindness and chose to join them. He had a few questions of his own.

MEMORY VERSE

'Do you not know that you are God's temple and that God's Spirit dwells in you?' (1 Cor. 3:16)

SUMMARY

The church is a people, not place. When Christians gather as the church, they pray, sing, and hear God's Word, all while remembering Jesus who died for them, rose for them, and one day soon will return to take them to be with Him forever.

WHAT'S THE POINT?
We go to church to grow with God and others.

2. WHY DO I HAVE TO GO TO CHURCH?

 BRIAN

Brian watched from the table as Dave filled cups of water and Ashley loaded plates with food. The conversation flowed casually and included lots of laughs, more than Brian was used to. Their questions seemed genuine, even refreshing.

Almost out of nowhere, Brian quipped, 'Do you guys really go to church every Sunday?' Dave smiled and explained that unless they were sick or something strange came up, they gathered with the church every Sunday. They'd done this since they became Christians.

'Okay, but do you *have to go to church* every Sunday?' Brian asked. They replied: 'God does command us to gather with other Christians, but even if He didn't, we love to go.' This seemed strange to Brian, but deep down it made sense. He asked if they would explain a little more, and they were happy to.

STOP

Have you ever wondered if God really wants you to go to church? And if He does, why? What questions do you have about why people go to church?

As you study this section, take time to write down thoughts that stand out to you and talk it over with a Christian friend.

The Bible tells us Jesus was raised from the dead on 'the first day of the week,' which would have been a Sunday (Matt. 28:1; Mark 16:2; Luke 24:1; John 20:1). Since then, Christians throughout the world have gathered on Sundays to celebrate Jesus' resurrection. They gather amid peace and persecution because God has transformed their lives.

As churches gather, they put God's love on display.

The following passage is a scene from the life of the first church. Their sins had led to Jesus' crucifixion, but His salvation had transformed their lives (Acts 2:22-41). As you read, notice what the church did because of their new relationship with Jesus.

'And they devoted themselves to the apostles' teaching and the fellowship, to the breaking of bread and the prayers. And awe came upon every soul, and many wonders and signs were being done through the apostles. And all who believed were together and had all things in common. And they were selling their possessions and belongings and distributing the proceeds to all, as any had need. And day by day, attending the temple together and breaking bread in their homes, they received their food with glad and generous hearts, praising God and having favour with all the people. And the Lord added to their number day by day those who were being saved.' – The Doctor Luke (Acts 2:42-47)

> **STOP**
>
> What marked this early church? What did they spend their time doing? How did they care for each other?

I hope you noticed that this church was not a spiritual social club. These former Christ-crucifers had been transformed into an assembly of Christ-worshippers. God had given them new life, which changed everything.

In this chapter we'll reflect on *five reasons* God calls His people to gather every week. Let's get started.

1. GOD'S PEOPLE GATHER TO WORSHIP GOD.

The church is made up of people who have been transformed by the living God through His inspired Word recorded in the Bible. In Acts 2, these brand-new baptized believers (2:38) devoted themselves to

prayer,

the apostles' teaching,

and the Lord's Supper (2:42).

They were in awe of God's power (2:43)

and praised Him with glad and sincere hearts (2:46-47).

Those elements make up the gatherings of a healthy church.

Christians gather on Sundays to hear God's Word taught so they can learn how to better obey Jesus and love others. They pray by

confessing their sins,

thanking God for what He has done,

and asking Him to do more.

They praise God, often through singing or testimonies.

They also share in the Lord's Supper together as a way to remember Jesus' sacrifice on their behalf.

Singing songs to God seems quite foreign to many new Christians. If this is true for you, it may be helpful to think about how singing works in the life of a church.

Paul calls the Ephesian church to worship by *addressing one another in psalms and hymns and spiritual songs, singing and making melody to the Lord with your heart* (Eph. 5:19).

> Singing serves *as a prayer* in which we lift our voices to God, praising Him for who He is and what He has done.

> Singing also serves *as a sermon* in which we direct the words about God to 'one another.'

> Finally, singing serves *as a personal testimony* in which we proclaim what we believe about God from our hearts.

God takes great delight when His people gather in faith to worship Him for all He has done for them in Jesus (Ps. 149:4).

2. GOD'S PEOPLE GATHER TO RECEIVE GOD'S WORD.

God's Word teaches us how to worship Him. In Acts 2:42 we see that *they devoted themselves to the apostles' teaching.* These people had experienced the power of God's Word when the Spirit used it to give them new life. They'd been born again and God's Word fed their spiritual appetite.

The apostles knew Jesus personally, and had been sent to teach people what it meant to follow Him. Though we don't have the apostles around today, we still have their Holy Spirit-inspired teachings preserved in the Bible.

We go to church to hear the Bible read (1 Tim. 4:13) and to hear pastors explain what it means and how it applies (Rom. 12:4-8). The early Church was committed to consuming this life-giving teaching. They were a people of the Word, and we should follow in their footsteps.

 ILLUSTRATION

My friend John used to deal cocaine, but God used a sermon from John 3 to save him. Before John was a Christian, he never read books, but in his first two years as a Christian, he read the entire Bible five times.

Why would a former drug dealer be so devoted to a book? Because he knows that the Bible isn't just any book. It contains God's very words.

Here's what happened in the church in **Acts 2**: new believers had been saved from their sins and were seeking to learn more about God. We should do the same.

Our gatherings reflect our need to hear from God.

We read God's Word and pray God's Word and sing God's Word and preach God's Word together as His people.

 BRIAN

At this point, Brian stopped the conversation and asked a question. *'I know I should want to hear God's Word, but what if I don't? Should I still go to church?'*

Now that's a good question. What would you say to Brian?

Dave and Ashley explained that the best thing to do when we feel like that is to read and listen to God's Word anyway. Let me explain.

ILLUSTRATION

When we become physically hungry, our belly growls, our body shakes, and some of us get grumpy. But then we eat, and the hunger is satisfied. Our body gets what it needs and we're filled.

Spiritual hunger works exactly the opposite way.

When we consume spiritual food through prayer and receiving God's Word our appetite is stirred up rather than suppressed. So, when we have no desire to read the Scriptures, we plead with God to help us, and then we open the Bible and read in faith believing that God will draw near to us as we draw near to Him.

We come to church to learn God's Word when we feel like it and when we don't, trusting that His Word gives us life.

3. GOD'S PEOPLE GATHER TO LOVE AND SERVE EACH OTHER.

'A new command I give you: Love one another. As I have loved you, so you must love one another. By this all men will know that you are my disciples, if you love one another.' (John 13:34-35, NIV)

A relationship with Jesus transforms the way we look at every aspect of life, especially how we think about other people. God frees us from using people and empowers us to love and serve them. So, when we gather as a church, we develop the types of relationships in which God's love is made visible (1 John 4:9-12).

The Acts 2 church was marked by servant-hearted love. Their love wasn't fake. As they gathered, they were told by God how to love one another. They ate meals together; they laughed together, cried together, celebrated together, and shared the ways God was at work among them. During these conversations, they became aware of needs and did whatever they could to meet those needs.

In Acts 2:44-46, we find a community of people who practically and sacrificially loved each other. If someone was in need, they weren't in need for long, because they were a body, a family. In other words, they were a church. This kind of sacrificial, practical love is a chief mark of someone who's been born again, as well as every healthy church.

ILLUSTRATION

In Ephesians 4:28 (NIV) Paul tells the church that, *'He who has been stealing must steal no longer, but must work, doing something useful with his own hands, that he may have something to share with those in need.'*

When a thief gets saved, he stops stealing. But he doesn't just stop stealing, he gets a job. But he doesn't just get a job to stockpile for himself, he works so he can share with others who might have needs. That's real transformation!

Christians gather as a church to develop relationships. Former sinners who used people have been transformed into servants who love others. This community is characterized by the kind of love Jesus showed us (1 John 3:16-18).

STOP

How does not going to church affect your ability to be loved by other Christians?

How does neglecting to go affect your ability to love others?

What would have happened if Dave and Ashley had just decided not to go to church that Sunday? God certainly would have cared for Brian in other ways, but he would have missed out on their love.

4. GOD'S PEOPLE GATHER TO FIGHT SIN TOGETHER.

'Take care, brothers, lest there be in any of you an evil, unbelieving heart, leading you to fall away from the living God. Exhort one

another every day, as long as it is called "today," that none of you may be hardened by the deceitfulness of sin' (Heb. 3:12-13).

The letter to the Hebrews was written to a congregation who was under great pressure to leave Jesus and return to their old lives. Coming to Jesus had been costly. Friends had turned their backs on them. Family members had disowned them. Employers had fired them. Temptations to sin swirled all around.

God has made the church a refuge for His people. In the community of believers, God provides the kind of relationships that help us keep following Jesus. The heat of persecution and the lure of temptation constantly bombard the believer, but the church rallies together as each member continues in faith toward heaven.

 ILLUSTRATION

I've never been to war, but I have friends who have. One of the most basic elements of warfare is that you don't go into the battle alone. You need fellow soldiers to encourage you, watch your back, and carry you if you're wounded. Following Jesus is a spiritual battle in which we need others to help us fight against sin.

This is why the author of Hebrews told the church to 'take care.' They were to be on guard, watching out with a non-stop attentiveness for the dangers that lurked. The church needed to take care of itself as a whole, but there was equal concern for every individual member.

What did they need to be careful for?

They needed to make sure their hearts didn't grow cold toward God, which would lead them to stop following God's ways. Our hearts are fickle and prone to being tricked. This is why we're called to *'exhort one another every day.'* The church has a daily responsibility to encourage each other to resist the lies of sin. Part of what it means to be a Christian is that you're regularly being exhorted *and* that you're regularly exhorting others to follow Jesus.

We should be relentless in exhorting one another because sin is relentless in its deception. Sin appears harmless, but like carbon monoxide that can fill a house undetected, it slowly kills your spiritual life by hardening your heart toward God. It begins small, but over time, it swallows you. Thankfully, God uses fellow believers to keep our hearts soft toward God, which enables us to persevere to the end and inherit salvation.

BRIAN

Over the next few days Brian talked with his buddies about church. Rather than encourage him, they assured him that church would brainwash him and make him snooty. He felt the pressure to leave what he'd heard behind. But the night before church, he got a text message from Dave asking him to sit with them at church the next day. This helped Brian resolve to go again.

STOP

How important do you think it is to have Christian friends?
What are particular ways you are tempted to turn away from Jesus?
How could other Christians help you resist these temptations?

5. GOD'S PEOPLE GATHER TO BUILD EACH OTHER UP UNTIL WE SEE JESUS.

'Let us consider how to stir up one another to love and good works, not neglecting to meet together, as is the habit of some, but encouraging one another, and all the more as you see the Day drawing near.' (Heb. 10:24-25).

Many people come to church in the same way they come to a buffet or a shopping mall. They come as consumers with preferences they expect to be fulfilled. While we certainly should benefit from a church service, God has a much greater purpose. We gather to help others grow in their love for God and service to Him.

In these verses we find several commands that are to be continually applied. It lays out a mindset, a way the church should be thinking when they gather and scatter.

As Christians, God says we are to

> *consider* one another,
>
> *look at* one another,
>
> *think about* one another,
>
> *study* one another

—all in an effort to stir each other up to love and good deeds.

To 'stir up' means to do something in order to get a response. In a mean way, it's what I used to do to my little sister, provoking her to tears. As Christians, we do the exact opposite. We watch one another, not in a creepy way, but in a loving way that notices God's gifts and the opportunities we all have to use our gifts.

 ILLUSTRATION

Nancy was a widow. After her husband died, keeping the house in order became too much for her. So Jeremiah rallied members from our church to help. He arranged people to mow her lawn, organize belongings for a yard sale, get her finances in order, and a host of other practical needs. Jeremiah saw an opportunity for service, and he helped stir the church to love and good works.

God knows we need help in becoming more loving, more holy, more prone to doing good deeds. Love does not just *happen*. It must be encouraged and cultivated.

This is why we're warned 'not to neglect meeting together.' If we neglect assembling, love and good deeds among God's people will be slowed, personal spiritual growth will be stunted, evangelism will be stalled, and we may eventually fall away from following Jesus.

Hebrews offers severe warnings about our need to persevere in faith. It also highlights that gathering with the church is one of the ways God helps us persevere. This is why we should be 'encouraging one another all the more as you see the Day drawing near.'

What does the Bible mean by the 'Day'? It's the day when Jesus returns; it's our great hope. We 'love His appearing' (2 Tim. 4:8) and know that even now we're nearer to seeing Him than when we first believed (Rom. 13:11). This truth is the central focus for Christians. It's what guides our hopes and warms our hearts. We remind each other day after day that we are almost home.

But as the day of Jesus' return draws closer, Satan's opposition against the church increases. Jesus warned that before He comes 'many will fall away and betray one another and hate one another and many false prophets will arise and lead many astray. And because lawlessness will be increased, the love of many will grow cold' (Matt. 24:10-12).

Satan does all he can to hinder Christians from continuing to follow Jesus. One of his schemes is to cool love between Christians. He seeks to stir division and dislike for each other.

But God calls us to resist the tempter by having an ever-increasing urgency and intensity in our love for one another. This sort of love and spiritual maturity is cultivated by being actively involved in a healthy local church.

STOP

What surprises you about God's plan for using the local church to help people obey Jesus?

How could a healthy church help you follow Jesus' teachings and example?

What questions do you still have regarding the importance of going to church?

BRIAN

He wasn't sure why, but as Brian heard Dave and Ashley describe the love of the early church, he began to tear up. While sitting at their table, he felt as if this church in Acts 2 was coming to life before his very eyes. God was providing a meal for him, but more importantly, He was introducing him to a new family—who would really love him and help him walk with God.

MEMORY VERSE

'Let us consider how to stir up one another to love and good works, not neglecting to meet together, as is the habit of some, but encouraging one another, and all the more as you see the Day drawing near' (Heb. 10:24-25).

SUMMARY

Though we may not always 'feel like it', Christians go to church regularly, to strengthen and be strengthened by fellowship with other Christians, to hear God's Word preached, and to praise Him in response.

WHAT'S THE POINT?

What to look for in a church.

3. WHAT IS A TRUE CHURCH?

 BRIAN

Brian began noticing churches around town. He had seen them before, but never given them much thought. There were 'first' churches and 'united' churches. There were Methodist churches and Baptist churches—Catholic churches and Mormon tabernacles. There were trendy churches and traditional ones.

All this left Brian confused. So he did what he always did when he had a question, he texted Dave.'Why are there so many churches? Don't we all believe in the same God?'

Dave laughed and responded that they should have that conversation in person.

The next day at breakfast, Dave encouraged Brian for asking such a good question. He explained that it would probably be helpful to try to answer in two parts.

First, they agreed to sort through the difference between a true and false church. Not every group who call themselves Christians really are, and knowing the difference is essential. Second, they chose to talk about why there were so many different types of true Christian churches. Though Christians believe the same basic truths, there are some matters of conviction that lead faithful believers to part ways, hopefully in a peaceful manner.

We'll take the first part in this chapter and the second part in the following one.

BEWARE OF FALSE TEACHERS

'Beware of false prophets, who come to you in sheep's clothing but inwardly are ravenous wolves. You will recognize them by their fruits. Are grapes gathered from thornbushes, or figs from thistles? So, every healthy tree bears good fruit, but the diseased tree bears bad fruit. A healthy tree cannot bear bad fruit, nor can a diseased tree bear good fruit. Every tree that does not bear good fruit is cut down and thrown into the fire. Thus you will recognize them by their fruits' (Matt. 7:15-20).

Jesus warned that false teachers were coming.

These deceitful guides make their way into churches and distort the truth (Jude 4).

> They twist God's Word and tell people what they want to hear (1 Tim. 6:5; 2 Tim. 4:3-4).

They peddle a false gospel that promotes immorality, and they misuse authority to take advantage of Jesus' bride (2 Pet. 2:1-3).

False teachers are wolves that disguise themselves in Christian-sounding language. They *appear* to follow God, but they don't. They lead churches that *talk* about God and the gospel. But in reality, they speak of a false god and a false gospel.

So how can we tell true churches from false ones?

Jesus tells us: 'by their fruits.' As we search the Scriptures, we find there are three characteristics that mark a true church. When these characteristics are absent, you can be confident you're looking at a false church.

Enough with the preamble. Three marks of a true church are as follows: the preaching of the pure gospel, the right administration of baptism and the Lord's Supper, and the guarding of the church's holiness through church discipline.

1. PREACH THE PURE GOSPEL

'The time is fulfilled, and the kingdom of God is at hand; repent and believe in the gospel' – Jesus (Mark 1:15).

Jesus preached the good news of God's kingdom from the beginning to the end of His earthly ministry.

After His resurrection, He charged His disciples to do the same (see chapter 9 for more on this). The good news that Jesus died in our place and rose for our justification is the bedrock on which all believers rest their eternal destiny.

If a church doesn't preach this good news, then it's not a true church.

Jesus said that unless someone builds their lives upon Him and obedience to His teaching, they are building on sand that will not hold on the Day of Judgment (Matt. 7:24-27). Paul said the gospel was of 'first importance' when writing to the Corinthian church (1 Cor. 15:1-5). This is vital because 'the gospel is the power of God for salvation to all who believe' (Rom. 1:16).

ILLUSTRATION

Imagine you're in the mood for a steak dinner. You and your buddies load up and drive to a local steakhouse. When you arrive, everything looks great. There are pictures of cows on the wall, sharp knives on the table, and mouthwatering smells fill the air.

But what happens if the server delivers the food and you find your plate filled with a slab of tofu? You would certainly have lots of thoughts, but one of them would surely be, 'This is no steakhouse!'

Sadly this is the same scenario people go through when they visit many churches today. They come hoping to be fed by God's Word, but instead they get served cotton candy.

BRIAN

Brian understood that having the gospel was essential for a true church, but he wasn't sure exactly what to watch for. So he asked, 'What should I listen for to know if a church is preaching the true gospel?'

Dave explained that it required discernment, but he suggested four things.

1. They must preach the true God.

The true God is presented to us in the true gospel. The God of the Bible is one God who has eternally existed as three distinct persons—

God the Father,

God the Son,

and God the Holy Spirit.

While this truth is mysterious, it must never be denied.

Some false churches will deny it. For instance,

Mormons believe that our God is one among many gods.

Jehovah's Witnesses deny that Jesus is God.

Oneness Pentecostals deny the Trinitarian nature of God.

Any supposed gospel that points you to believe in a false god is a false gospel. True churches honour God by presenting Him as He has revealed Himself in Scripture.

2. *They must preach about sin.*

Many churches today aim to make people feel good about themselves at great cost. But the Bible is very clear that all of us have sinned gravely against a holy God by disobeying His Law (Rom. 3:10-18, 23). This sin is serious and leads to spiritual, physical, and eternal death (Rom. 6:23).

To make light of our rebellion against God is dangerous and deceptive.

True churches will aim to help people see their standing before a holy God in light of what He says in the Bible. Their aim is *not* to make people feel bad, but to alert them in love of their need to be forgiven and God's provision of forgiveness through Jesus (Isa. 1:18).

3. *They must preach grace alone through faith alone in Christ alone.*

Any gospel that tempts us to trust in our own good works to appease God is a false gospel. One of the most tragic errors that plagues the church is a works-based gospel. This supposed gospel says Jesus is important, but to be accepted by God we must also have some combination of church attendance, baptism, good works, financial gifts, and the list goes on and on.

The gospel that saves declares without shame that forgiveness of our sins is an undeserved, unearned gift from God.

It's by grace alone. It can be accepted only by trusting in what Jesus has done on our behalf. It's received by faith alone, and the focus of our faith is completely on the perfect life, substitutionary death, and bodily resurrection of Jesus. It's in Christ alone.

 'For by grace you have been saved through faith. And this is not your own doing; it is the gift of God, not a result of works, so that no one may boast' (Eph. 2:8-9).

The true Gospel gives God all the glory because on that last day, no one will strut into heaven on their own merit. Anyone who withstands God's judgment will do so not because they were perfect, but because Jesus was perfect in their place. A gospel that adds anything to the work of Jesus is no gospel at all, but rather a dangerous lie that leads people to condemnation (Gal. 1:8-9).

4. They must preach the need for repentance.

Any Gospel that does not radically affect the way we live is a false gospel.

This is why Jesus said, '*If anyone would come after Me, let him deny himself and take up his cross daily and follow Me*' (Luke 9:23). To follow Him in faith requires the death of following our old sinful ways.

In other words, faith and repentance are two sides of the same coin. To follow Jesus, we must turn away from our sinful life and turn toward Him and His ways. This turning is what the Bible calls repentance.

Sadly, many churches today promote a false idea that if you simply pray a prayer to God, walk an aisle at church, or make some sort of public profession, then nothing more is required. This couldn't be further from the truth.

The Bible teaches that when we are united to Jesus by faith, we are justified (declared righteous) in God's sight. That justification is evidenced by acts of faith and obedience that prove we are indeed born again. This transformation may be slow and will include failures, but if we are new creatures, there will be evidence. Striving by faith to please God all the way to the end must mark the life of a believer. Any gospel that doesn't call you to obey God is a false gospel.

STOP

As you have been to churches, have you heard these essential elements of faithful teaching?

Why do you think a church must be clear on each of these elements? What happens if they are not?

Any church that claims to represent Jesus but doesn't believe, proclaim, and defend the good news of Jesus is a false church. On the other hand, any church that declares, delights in, and contends for the gospel is a true church.

Of all the marks of a true church, this first one is the most important. What follows are implications of the first one. If the Word is being taught correctly, it will serve to rightly shape every other part of the church's life. But if it is being taught incorrectly, everything else will undoubtedly suffer.

2. FAITHFULLY ADMINISTER BAPTISM AND THE LORD'S SUPPER

'We were buried therefore with Him by baptism into death, in order that, just as Christ was raised from the dead by the glory of the Father, we too might walk in newness of life' (Rom. 6:4).

Jesus gave His church baptism and the Lord's Supper as ordinances—some call them 'sacraments'—that are to be administered faithfully according to His Word. An ordinance is a religious ritual that serves as a symbol, or illustration, of the gospel message. Baptism symbolizes our new birth through Jesus while the Lord's Supper pictures our on-going communion with Jesus.

In chapter seven we'll explore how baptism and the Lord's Supper fit into the life of the church, but here we will highlight two ways true churches administer these ordinances.

1. They must be done in accordance with gospel preaching.

The ordinances make the audible word of the gospel visible. When someone is baptized, we're given a picture of what happens when a sinner is united to Jesus by faith. Similarly, when we partake of the Lord's Supper, we partake of physical symbols that remind us of Jesus' body and blood that were given for our sins.

Neither baptism nor the Lord's Supper should be performed in a way that separates them from the finished work of Jesus. Being baptized doesn't make us acceptable to God. It doesn't give us any kind of justifying grace. Instead,

> **baptism serves as a physical symbol of the spiritual reality that a sinner has been made alive by Jesus.**

In the same way, partaking of the bread and the cup in the Lord's Supper should never be viewed as giving any sort of grace that ensures our standing before God. We can add nothing to the finished work of Jesus. Rather, the Lord's Supper is intended to be a sober celebration of faith that rejoices in Jesus' death on our behalf. Indeed this is what Jesus taught when He said 'Do this in remembrance of me' (1 Cor. 11:24-25).

True churches celebrate the ordinances as illustrations of the gospel; false churches often turn them into a way to earn our standing before God.

2. They must be participated in by faith.

Baptism and the Lord's Supper are intended to stir the heart of a believer toward faith and enjoyment of God. Because of this, they must always be partaken by those who have faith.

> **One way false churches abuse the ordinances is by inviting unbelievers to partake in them.**

For instance, there's a church near me that boasts in allowing anyone to come to the Lord's Supper. As they say, 'All are welcomed, no questions asked.' Their invitation appears loving, but it's not. Reducing the Lord's Supper exclusively to a symbol of inclusion that requires no repentance or faith is blasphemy that incites God's judgment.

The ordinances serve as visible pictures of the gospel, and they must be administered as servants to the gospel message. They're never intended to undermine the gravity of the gospel; instead they uphold it for the church as they partake together.

True churches administer the ordinances according to the Bible's command; false churches use them to further their social, political, or humanistic agendas.

ILLUSTRATION

Ben and Jill were preparing to celebrate their 20-year anniversary. Ben bought cards and wrote Jill sweet poems about love. He cleaned his wedding ring and recited his vows in the mirror. He got a fresh haircut and dressed up in a new suit. He cooked a fancy dinner and put champagne on ice while romantic music filled the air.

While it may appear that Ben was crushing it, there was a problem. Ben never talked to his wife the whole day. The cards were kept in his drawer. He never held her hand or looked her in the eyes. He never even said a single word to her. If you were Ben's wife, what would you say to him? You might say that all the stuff he did was absolutely meaningless because it really had nothing to do with her at all. He seemed to love the idea of the anniversary more than his wife.

This is strikingly similar to a church that goes through rituals apart from gospel truth and living faith. True churches strive to observe the ordinances as an act of worship, not as an end in themselves.

BRIAN

As Dave described the meaning behind the ordinances, Brian was deeply encouraged. He grew up around people who did religious rituals, but had no love for God. Though he had no love for God at the time, their pious pretending annoyed Brian. To hear that God was displeased with such behaviour brought Brian peace. The more he listened, the more he desired to be a part of a church that didn't just go through the motions, but that truly loved God.

STOP

Why do you think God has given visible illustrations of the gospel for us?

How can rightly taking the ordinances help your faith in Jesus grow?

Why do you think some churches end up performing empty rituals rather than resting in Jesus' finished work?

3. PRACTICE PURIFYING CHURCH DISCIPLINE

'As obedient children, do not be conformed to the passions of your former ignorance, but as he who called you is holy, you also be holy in all your conduct, since it is written, "You shall be holy, for I am holy"' (1 Pet. 1:14-16).

When God saves people, He calls them into His body, the church. The church is to be a corporate display of His character. This means

a true church is a holy church.

As we saw in chapter 1, the word 'holy' means to be set apart. The church is called to be set apart from sin, and set apart to God. A church's holiness is seen most basically in love and obedience to God (John 14:15) and

love for one another (John 13:34-35).

A true church strives to fight sin together. Because they love God and desire Him to be honoured, they will confess their sins and repent of them diligently. A false church doesn't really care about holiness. They're content to have moral lessons that apply to everyone generally, but real accountability is viewed as intrusive and judgmental. False churches also care about holiness for the wrong reasons. Perhaps they see good deeds as the way we're made right before God.

Because Jesus desires His church to be holy, He instituted a practice called church discipline (Matt. 18:15-20). Church discipline refers to the way church members hold each other accountable to God's Word. There are several steps in the process, but in the end, it can result in someone being removed from membership in a local church.

The aim of this sort of intrusive love is to reconcile straying believers to God and to the church. As with the ordinances, we will cover church discipline more in a future chapter (ch. 8), but for now, let's consider two reasons discipline must be present in a true church.

1. Church discipline guards the reputation of Jesus.

Of all the things that give Jesus and His church a bad name, hypocrisy is near the top of the list. I've heard countless unbelievers reject ideas from the Bible because of 'all the hypocrites' that fill churches. Some of Jesus' strongest words were against religious hypocrites who pretended to know God but lived as if they did not (Matt. 7:5, 15:7, 23:1-39). True churches, however, care what people think about God, so they practice church discipline to guard His name.

2. Church discipline guards the souls of people.

When a church confronts sin in a person's life, it has a sobering effect on everyone involved.

> For the person who's straying, it alerts them to the danger that comes from giving in to sin's temptations (James 5:19-20).

> For the people who are aiming to help the straying sinner, it brings a reminder to be on guard against their own weaknesses (Gal. 6:1-2).

> For the church as a whole, it humbles them by reminding them of how susceptible we all are to sin's deceitfulness (1 Tim. 5:20).

> And finally, confronting sin serves as a witness to all that there is indeed a day of final judgment coming and that we must deal with our sin today, before it is too late (1 Cor. 5:1-13).

A false church isn't concerned with God's glory or helping people avoid the final judgment. That sort of environment is a dangerous place for any person's soul. A true church knows that God's Word must not only be proclaimed, but it must be received and applied in faith. Part of that application is the practice of church discipline.

STOP

Have you ever been around religious hypocrites? If so, how did they affect the way you viewed God and what He says in the Bible? Have you ever been in a church that cares enough to hold each other accountable for the way they live?

If the church members who do this are aware of how much Jesus has forgiven them, how do you think that would affect the way they carried out this accountability?

BRIAN

Brian was amazed to learn that some churches weren't actually churches at all. This stirred a strange mixture of sadness and anger. He was also thankful to know that the church he and Dave attended seemed to care about things God cared about. But that got him thinking about the second part of his question: why are there so many different kinds of true churches?

MEMORY VERSE

'Beware of false prophets, who come to you in sheep's clothing but inwardly are ravenous wolves. You will recognize them by their fruits. Are grapes gathered from thornbushes, or figs from thistles? So, every healthy tree bears good fruit, but the diseased tree bears bad fruit' (Matt. 7:15-20).

SUMMARY

Seeking to discern what marks a true church isn't an arrogant endeavour. Rather, it's a response of humility, faith, and love. It's humble because it surrenders to God's will and God's Word. It's faithful because it forces us to act on what God has revealed. And it's loving because it orients our thoughts and actions rightly toward both God and neighbour.

WHAT'S THE POINT?
United in love despite our differences.

4. WHY ARE THERE SO MANY DIFFERENT CHURCHES?

BRIAN

The difference between a true church and a false church made sense to Brian. But he was still confused as to why so many true churches gathered separately. He admitted that he might be a little naïve, but couldn't understand why churches who loved the same God and believed the same Bible would disagree enough to not worship together.

STOP

Why do you think there are so many different churches?
What bad reasons might Christians have for worshipping separately?
Can you think of any good reasons?
Do you think God is pleased with the great variety of churches? Why or why not?

'I do not ask for these only, but also for those who will believe in me through their word, that they may all be one, just as you, Father, are in me, and I in you, that they also may be in us, so that the world may believe that you have sent me.' – Jesus (John 17:20-21)

Before Jesus went to the cross, He prayed that His church would be unified. The church's oneness serves as a witness to the world that Jesus is God's Son. This unity was purchased by His blood (Eph. 2:13-16) and must be eagerly maintained by His people (Eph. 4:1-6).

And yet, when we look at the landscape of the modern church, we find hundreds or even thousands of denominations. The Merriam-Webster Dictionary defines a denomination as '*a religious organization whose congregations are united in their adherence to its beliefs and practices.*' While all true Christian churches hold the most basic truths about God and salvation in common, they often have differing convictions about other aspects of doctrine and worship.

Before we talk about some of the doctrinal issues that may lead churches to worship separately, let's take a moment to consider how the church went from being one unified church to the diversity of churches we see today.

A BRIEF HISTORY LESSON

The church was established when God sent the Holy Spirit to indwell His people (Acts 2:1-13). As the gospel spread through-out the known world, many local churches were established (Acts 2-28). The New Testament letters (Romans through Revelation) were written to help these churches apply the teaching of Jesus and His Apostles.

The early Church endured much persecution from political powers and false teachers. Splinter groups of false churches such as Gnostics (mystic dualism), Arians (denied Jesus was God), and Marcionites (said the God of the Old Testament and God of the New Testament were different) were always a threat, yet God preserved His true church, just as Jesus promised (Matt. 16:18).

In these early centuries, councils of church leaders developed formal statements that clarified what the church believed. These councils did not make up new doctrines; rather, they sought to summarize what the church had always believed in ways that would protect the church from false teaching. These statements are known today as creeds and are still helpful for Christian churches.

The true church generally remained unified until the eleventh century when the 'Great Schism' occurred, splitting the Eastern (Orthodox) and Western (Roman Catholic) church. This division had many factors, culminating in controversies about the authority of the pope and God the Holy Spirit's relationship with God the Father and God the Son.

In the 16th Century, several movements began calling into question the corrupted faith and practice of the Roman Catholic Church. These protestors and their sympathizers became known as Protestants and emerged in four major groups known generally as the Lutheran, Swiss, English, and Anabaptist reformers.

While these churches agreed strongly on foundational doctrines of salvation, they differed in conviction over other important issues. This led to the development of other groups such as

Methodists,

Presbyterians,

Episcopalians,

Congregationalists,

and Baptists.

Since then, there have been splits, schisms, divisions, and theological disagreements, yet the vast majority of Protestant churches remain unified in the key tenets of the Christian faith.

BRIAN

After hearing how God had built His church over the centuries, Brian felt like he needed more clarity on reasons churches might decide to divide. Dave gave four suggestions.

1. NECESSITY

The most basic reason all Christians do not meet together is that it is not possible. Christians are geographically spread throughout communities, regions, states, nations, and continents. While this may seem obvious, it's helpful to point out that the early church often had various gatherings of believers in the same region.

For instance, the letter known as Galatians was written 'to the churches of Galatia' (Gal. 1:2). We don't know how many churches were in the region, but they did not all gather together, though they apparently knew of each other. Similarly, letters like 1 Peter (1:1), James (1:1), and Revelation (1:4, 2:1–3:22) are clearly addressed to like-minded churches who were unable to meet all at once because of their geographic location.

Another reason churches may not meet together is due to language barriers. While a church may choose to use interpreters to bridge the language divide, it's often prudent to plant congregations that allow members to worship God in their mother tongue.

Sometimes, separate gatherings are based on necessity, not sinful division.

2. DOCTRINAL CONVICTIONS

As we mentioned in the summary of church history, most denominations form because of different convictions over specific doctrines. A doctrine is a summary of what the Bible teaches on a particular issue such as baptism, spiritual gifts, or how church leadership should be organized.

The Apostle Paul describes the kind of division that can take place:

'One person esteems one day as better than another, while another esteems all days alike. Each one should be fully convinced in his own mind' (Rom. 14:5).

An example today is baptism.

Some Christians believe that baptizing infants marks their children with the sign of the covenant community in the same way circumcision was given to children under the Abrahamic Covenant (Gen. 17:7-8; Acts 16:32-34). Other believers believe that baptism is reserved only for believers as the sign of the New Covenant (Matt. 28:18-20; Rom. 6:1-4; Col. 2:11-12). This disagreement is significant enough to lead people to worship at different churches, but not significant enough to break loving fellowship. We'll discuss this a little further in the next chapter.

The Bible teaches that while all believers are united in foundational issues (Eph. 4:1-6), we may have deeply rooted convictions in secondary issues such as this one (Rom. 14:1-23; 1 Cor. 8:1-13). These matters of conviction must be followed in faith, 'for whatever does not proceed from faith is sin' (Rom. 14:23).

 ILLUSTRATION

Here are seven of the most common doctrinal issues true churches disagree on. Not all these issues must result in a church breaking fellowship, but every congregation must prayerfully seek how they are to please the Lord.

1. Baptism.

Should children be baptized as a sign of the covenant? Or is it only for professing believers following conversion?

Can baptism be done by pouring, sprinkling, or only by immersion?

2. Lord's Supper.

Can only members of your church take the Lord's Supper or can any Christian?

Is the Lord's Supper only a memorial to remember Jesus? Or is it a spiritual communion with Him?

Should we only use unleavened bread and wine—or can we use rolls and grape juice?

3. Church Government.

Who has the authority in the church? Pastors? The Congregation? An outside group?

Can women serve as deacons? Can they serve as elders / pastors?

4. Doctrines of Grace.

How do God's sovereignty and people's responsibility fit together in salvation?

Can you lose your salvation? Or are believers sealed forever by the Holy Spirit?

5. End Times.

How will the events at the end of time unfold?

What is the relationship between Israel and the church?

6. *Spiritual Gifts.*

Are there some spiritual gifts—healing, prophecy, tongues—that are no longer given to the church today?

If they are still active, how should gifts like tongues and prophecy function in the church?

7. *Philosophy of Ministry.*

How should a church carry out its ministry?

Should a church have Sunday School? Small groups? Programs?

As you can see, there are many important topics believers will develop convictions about. As they do, they find themselves in groups with other like-minded believers. Some believers will feel more or less comfortable being in fellowship where there is disagreement, but we must always strive to live in harmony with one another (Rom. 12:16).

PERSONAL PREFERENCES

When it comes to reasons Christians choose to fellowship separately, this may be the most difficult to sort through. On the one hand, we're commanded to serve one another in love (Gal. 5:13), consider others more important than ourselves (Phil. 2:3-4), and not aim to please ourselves at the expense of others (Rom. 15:1).

On the other hand, there is nothing inherently wrong with choosing to worship with other believers who enjoy similar musical styles, liturgy forms, and cultural expressions. There are certain atmospheres and styles that feel more natural and comfortable for each of us.

We must remember: unity in Christ doesn't require uniformity in culture, style, and expression.

Diversity is a beautiful gift from God that reflects His Trinitarian nature. And yet, what we have in common with other churches is more important than what's unique about us. Some believers will have their souls stirred by the solemnity of a traditional Presbyterian church service in Boston; others will rejoice in the soulful worship of a Baptist church in Zambia.

BRIAN

Brian stopped Dave, *'Okay, but aren't there dangers in just picking a church based on what I want? That seems like it could develop a selfish way of thinking.'*

Dave agreed and suggested a couple ideas to keep in mind.

1. Be careful not to pursue preferences at the expense of truth.
Pray for God to help you find a faithful church where you feel at home, but be careful to not compromise truth in favour of preferences. Faithful teaching is always the most important element of a church. Sadly, many churches offer strong culture or dynamic experiences, yet neglect faithful teaching of the Bible. This is a trade-off you can't afford.

ILLUSTRATION

As a young believer, I attended a small church. This group had a particular music style that nourished my soul. I found its soulful freedom liberating and edifying.

And yet, as I grew in my understanding of the Bible, I realized the church lacked faithful teaching. They used the Bible in ways that seemed strange. This led me to visit other churches. To my dismay, I found good teaching, but the musical worship was stifling.

I was tempted to attend various churches to get the best of both worlds, but a wise friend counselled me to find a place that faithfully taught the Word and serve there. Looking back, I'm grateful for that advice. God used it to protect me from having a low view of the Bible.

2. Be careful to not pursue preferences at the expense of others.

The church doesn't exist simply to serve our needs and desires. Christians follow Jesus who did not come to be served, but to serve (Mark 10:45). So, when searching for a church, we should ask God to show us how He might use us to bless others. God often calls us to serve Him in uncomfortable places, so we should be willing to follow Him and bless others anywhere He calls.

The call to serve doesn't mean we should *not* seek to be served by the preaching and members of our church. It does mean, however, that our attitude must always be that of a servant, not a consumer.

 'Do nothing from selfish ambition or conceit, but in humility count others more significant than yourselves. Let each of you look not only to his own interests, but also to the interests of others. Have this mind among yourselves, which is yours in Christ Jesus.' – The Apostle Paul (Phil. 2:3-5)

Preferences are an important part of finding a church home, but we must be careful to not justify a selfish decision at the expense of truth or service to others.

STOP

What are some of your meaningful preferences that could influence where you go to church?

What are ways you could be tempted to allow your preferences to become too big of a factor in your decision?

---

3. Sinful Splits

True believers can become ensnared in sinful attitudes that result in sinful divisions. They can allow preferences to become too prominent, they can hold grudges and leave, they can squabble over leadership decisions—the list could go on and on.

Sadly, there are many examples of this, even in the Bible. The clearest example is the church of Corinth. Now Corinth was a city known for its philosophers and perversions. The church had been infected by the world's values, which brought division. In particular, they become enamoured with particular teachers and so they formed cliques.

 'I appeal to you, brothers, by the name of our Lord Jesus Christ, that all of you agree, and that there be no divisions among you, but that you be united in the same mind and the same judgment. For it has been reported to me by Chloe's people that there is quarrelling among you, my brothers. What I mean is that each one of you says, "I follow Paul," or "I follow Apollos," or "I follow Cephas," or "I follow Christ."' (1 Cor. 1:10-12)

Believers should have an appropriate affection for their pastors and other leaders. But in the Corinthian church, things had gotten out of hand. Paul says they 'quarrelled' with each other over which teachers were the best. Instead of appreciating the gifts God had given to their teachers, they idolized them and formed cliques. This created a culture of comparison and personality worship.

This sort of division is sinful.

When believers allow affection for certain teachers, brands, denominations, or personalities to get out of control, they can make the sinful choice to belittle or part ways with other churches.

STOP

If gossip and complaining became prominent among certain members, what effect might that have on the church?

How could unforgiveness impact a church? What about disputes over money?

What other sins could hurt a church and lead to a split?

What might you be able to do if you hear someone gossiping about another church? How could you encourage that brother or sister to think differently?

BRIAN

Brian sat back and looked toward the ceiling: 'I wish churches could just worship together. This is what God wants, right?' Dave reached for his Bible and began turning toward the end. As he did, he said, 'What you're feeling is good. God *does* want His people to worship together—and when Jesus returns, we will.'

In Revelation 7:9-10, God gave the apostle John a vision of the church in the future. Listen to his description: '*I looked, and behold, a great multitude that no one could number, from every nation, from all tribes and peoples and languages, standing before the throne and before the Lamb, clothed in white robes, with palm branches in their hands, and crying out with a loud voice, "Salvation belongs to our God who sits on the throne, and to the Lamb!"*'

This is a snapshot of the unity God's church will know in eternity. A day is coming when there will be no more divisions or denominations. All believers will see clearly and faith will be needed no more—because we will be with Jesus.

That will be a wonderful day, but it hasn't happened yet.

Therefore today we must be '*eager to maintain the unity of the Spirit in the bond of peace*' (Eph. 4:3). After all, unity won't just happen. Our sinful tendencies and Satan's attacks always work against it.

But we know Jesus desires His church to be united as a witness of His greatness, so we must plead for His help.

Here are a few ways you might consider.

1. Ask God to give you a humble posture toward other churches.

We all see in a mirror dimly (1 Cor. 13:12). There's no one denomination or group of Christians who is completely right on every interpretation and application of the Bible. We should assume in our disagreements that we all have differing degrees of blindness.

This difficulty of spiritual blindness does *not* give us an excuse to be lazy in understanding God's Word. Instead, it ought to produce a posture of humility toward others. Just because someone is not in your church group doesn't mean they are not in the Lord's (Luke 9:49-50).

2. Ask God to help you speak of and act charitably toward other churches.

Be careful to not slander Jesus' bride with criticisms and complaints. Certainly she is an imperfect bride, but when speaking about your church or other churches, be careful not to tarnish their reputation. Remember that Jesus loves His church and we ought to strive to love her as well.

By being charitable, you'll open doors for dialogue that will honour God. It also guards the hearts of people in your church and unbelievers from thinking ill of other Christians.

STOP

Why do you think some believers struggle to speak well of other churches?

How might God use your encouragement and kind words about other churches to honour His name?

3. Pray for other churches.

We should always pray for our own church, but we can cultivate a spirit of unity by also praying for other churches by name. Whether you do this in your personal devotions, in a small group, or from the pulpit, praying for other churches greatly honours God.

Here are a few examples to help you get started:

God, bless them so they would know You and love You all the more.

God, help them to hate sin and love holiness.

God, guard their unity so they can better honour Your name.

God, bring revival in their midst. Use them, grow them, help them see conversions.

God, bless the preaching of Your Word there, and bless their pastor with power.

God, guard them from the evil one and help them to know Your protection.

Basically, anything you would want someone to pray for your church, pray for other local churches. Over time, this changes believers' hearts and puts the unity Jesus prayed for on display.

4. Seek ways to cooperate together in kingdom work.

While every church ought to be faithful with what God has called them to do, working together is often wise. Churches could cooperate to send missionaries or develop a gospel-centred homeless shelter. Opportunities for cooperation abound. While this can be challenging because churches can have differing convictions, it encourages us to learn from each other and put our Christ-centred unity on display.

ILLUSTRATION

I pastor a Baptist church outside Washington, D.C. We currently share our building with a Presbyterian church. While our churches differ on baptism, church government, and a few other things— we agree much more than we disagree. Our churches share a warm affection for each other and have partnered together in this season in a way that honours God, encourages our churches, and shows the world proof that Jesus is God's Son. We often receive comments from non-believing neighbours who see our unity as unique and compelling.

BRIAN

After learning more about God's purposes in our differences, Brian left encouraged by the diversity he saw in the churches around him. He understood that there would always be strife and misunderstanding, but the potential to put the gospel on display gave him reason to strive for unity with other believers.

MEMORY VERSE

'I appeal to you, brothers, by the name of our Lord Jesus Christ, that all of you agree, and that there be no divisions among you, but that you be united in the same mind and the same judgment' (1 Cor. 1:10-12).

SUMMARY

Differences provide an opportunity for the church to show the world what true unity really looks like. In a day when disagreement is perceived as hate, believers have an opportunity to show humble, charitable, kingdom-cooperating love. This sort of unity requires energy, effort, prayer, instruction, confession, and repentance, but it's worth it.

WHAT'S THE POINT?

Baptism and communion display our union with Jesus.

5. BAPTISM AND THE LORD'S SUPPER

 BRIAN

Dave and Ashley often hosted people for meals after church. During these meals, Brian was amazed how much God had changed his life. Not only did he sense a nearness to God, but he also began to care about people from church.

After about two months of attending Sunday services, Dave asked Brian what he thought about being baptized and becoming a member of the church. Brian asked Dave to explain a little more.

Dave grabbed his Bible and said, 'Let's start with what baptism and the Lord's Supper are, and then we'll talk about what it means to be a member of a church.' It sounded like a good plan.

In this chapter we'll take baptism and the Lord's Supper. Then in the next chapter we'll discuss church membership.

STOP

What do you think baptism and the Lord's Supper are?
What would motivate believers to be baptized and take the Supper together?

Jesus gave baptism and the Lord's Supper to His church as ordinances—sometimes, as we mentioned before, called 'sacraments'—to be administered as part of their worship. An 'ordinance' is something ordained or commanded by someone in authority—in this case God. A 'sacrament' is something sacred, or **set apart by God with special meaning**. Either word can be used, but I prefer 'ordinance' because it avoids confusion that these elements could have any kind of saving power.

Put simply:

> **the gospel proclaims that we are saved through faith alone in Jesus alone.**

In His kindness, God has prescribed these two practices to illustrate this good news.

 ILLUSTRATION

On our wedding day, my wife and I stood before a gathering of friends and family and proclaimed vows to each other. Those vows didn't *create* our marriage, but they served as a way to publicly swear off other lovers and promise to be faithful to each other as long as God gave us life. Even today, our vows serve as a constant reminder of the devotion we promised to each other and our accountability to all who heard us make those promises.

Baptism and the Lord's Supper serve the church in a similar way. Through baptism, a believer publicly professes their devotion to Jesus and His people. Through the Lord's Supper, we renew our vows of devotion by remembering Jesus' death, resurrection, and impending return.

Before we talk about baptism and the Lord's Supper in more detail, we should answer a few key questions about the ordinances.

Who created the idea of ordinances?

Jesus instituted baptism and the Lord's Supper. They're not merely religious rituals Christians dreamed up, but divinely designed symbols that serve both the church and watching world.

To whom did Jesus give the ordinances?

Jesus gave the ordinances to His church. In Matthew 16:18-19 and 18:18-20 Jesus gave His 'keys' of authority to the church to speak and act on His behalf. This does not mean the church saves people, but they do have the authority to represent Jesus.

What does this mean, practically?

It means local churches can say with confidence that a person will be forgiven of their sin if they repent and believe in Jesus. So, when someone comes to Christ, a church baptizes him because only the church has been given the authority to administer the ordinance of baptism as a sign to new believers. Similarly, only the church has been given the authority to administer the Lord's Supper to believers. As churches administer baptism and the Lord's Supper, they help draw loving lines that clarify who is in right standing with Jesus, and who is not.

 ILLUSTRATION

I'm a big football fan. I root for the perpetually underachieving Minnesota Vikings and my brother-in-law roots for the New York Jets (who are even worse). A few years back our teams played each other in New York. As I walked into the stadium wearing a Vikings jersey, stares, glares, and some of the most creative cursing I've heard came my way. I saw another group of Vikings fans being mobbed as police tried to intervene.

Our jerseys set us apart. Our allegiances were clear for all to see. In a similar way, this is what baptism and the Lord's Supper do.

They clearly mark us apart as belonging to Jesus. They publicly say, *'I am not ashamed to let you know I am with Jesus'* (Matt. 10:32-33).

Why did Jesus give Baptism and Lord's Supper?

God makes promises about how He will relate to His people. When God makes these promises, He gives a physical sign as a reminder to go with it.

God gave Noah the sign of a rainbow,

Abraham the sign of circumcision,

Moses the sign of Sabbath, and

David the sign of a throne.

When Jesus came, He fulfilled all of God's previous covenants and instituted the New Covenant (Heb. 10:1-18). What does God promise in the New Covenant? Listen to this—

'The days are coming, declares the LORD, when I will make a new covenant with the house of Israel and the house of Judah...I will put my law within them, and I will write it on their hearts. And I will be their God, and they shall be my people...I will forgive their iniquity, and I will remember their sin no more.' (Jer. 31:31-34)

Under the New Covenant

our hearts are circumcised by God's Spirit (Rom. 2:29; Col. 2:10-12),

His Law is written on our hearts (Heb. 10:16),

our sins are washed away,

and our spiritually dead hearts are replaced with hearts that love God (Ezek. 36:25-26).

When someone turns to Jesus and is born again, they are brought into the New Covenant. Baptism and the Lord's Supper serve as signs of this covenant. Taking these signs does not bring us into the covenant, but they serve as pictures of our death to sin and resurrection with Christ as well as our on-going fellowship with Him.

BRIAN

Brian was already encouraged by their discussion. He was amazed that God would forgive his sins and promise to remember them no more. But all the talk about covenants was a little abstract for Brian, so he asked Dave to tell him more about baptism.

BAPTISM

'Jesus came and said to them, "All authority in heaven and on earth has been given to me. Go therefore and make disciples of all nations, baptizing them in the name of the Father and of the Son and of the Holy Spirit, teaching them to observe all that I have commanded you. And behold, I am with you always, to the end of the age."' (Matt 28:18-20)

Before Jesus ascended to heaven, He commanded His disciples to make disciples from every nation until He returns (see chapter 9). When someone becomes a disciple by repenting of their sins and believing in Jesus, they're to be baptized. Baptism is therefore a command for individual Christians, but also for local churches.

Jesus commands the church to call new believers to make their profession of Jesus known to the world. When someone from the church baptizes a new believer, they represent the whole church in saying, 'We affirm God's saving work in your life and we will help you follow Him and expect you to help us follow Him as well.'

As one friend explained, baptism is 'going public' with your faith.

It's the way a new Christian says to the church, 'I've been united with Jesus. As Jesus died for my sin, I have died to my sin and will now live for Him.'

In this way, baptism serves as a physical picture of the spiritual reality of what happens when we're united to Jesus through faith.

ILLUSTRATION

Do you know how a pickle becomes a pickle? If you take a cucumber and immerse it in brine (vinegar, water, and salt), something miraculous happens. As it's submerged, it takes on the properties of the brine and it becomes a pickle. The cucumber has been united with the brine in an irreversible way that actually transforms it into something new.

This pickling process is a good picture of what happens in spiritual baptism. Galatians 3:27 explains that through faith we are united with Jesus, 'as many of you as were baptized into Christ have put on Christ.' Our union with Him transforms us from a spiritually dead sinner opposed to God, to a living child of God who now flees from the sin we once loved. Romans 6 explains this reality beautifully.

'We were buried therefore with him by baptism into death, in order that, just as Christ was raised from the dead by the glory of the Father, we too might walk in newness of life. For if we have been united with him in a death like his, we shall certainly be united with him in a resurrection like his' (Rom. 6:4-5).

This passage gives us the story behind the story. When someone is united with Jesus through faith, everything that's true of Jesus becomes true of them. His death becomes their death to sin. His resurrection becomes their everlasting life.

Being united with Jesus changes them forever.

Put simply, water baptism is a picture of the spiritual baptism that not only unites us with Jesus, but also with His body, the church. First Corinthians 12:13 says *'in one Spirit we were all baptized into one body—Jews or Greeks, slaves or free—and all were made to drink of one Spirit.'* The Holy Spirit gives us hearts to believe in Jesus, which unites us with Him and with His body, the church.

BRIAN

So Dave said to Brian, *'If you were to be baptized, you'd be telling the church and the world that you are now following Jesus, you'd be committing to help us follow Jesus, and we'd be committing to help you.'* Brian believed what Dave had explained was true and said he desired to tell everyone how Jesus had changed His life. After a little more discussion, Brian had a few lingering questions.

Where should I get baptized?

The location of your baptism isn't as important as who is present to watch it. A baptism should happen in a time and place where the whole church can gather. So a church baptismal, a back yard pool, a river, or an ocean are all fine; what matters more is that the church is invited to participate.

Who should baptize me?

The Bible does not specify. Some churches allow anyone to perform the baptism citing the priesthood of all believers (1 Pet. 2:4-9), while others prefer elders or pastors to act as representatives of the whole church. As long as your baptism is done in accordance with the true gospel of Jesus, it will serve its purpose of illustrating your union with Him.

Is there a right way to be baptized?

The word baptism literally means 'to dip or immerse.' The picture in Romans 6 is one of dying and rising, and whenever baptism appears in the New Testament it describes people going down into and coming up out of water (Mark 1:10; Acts 8:38).

These factors lead us to believe that immersion is the proper way to be baptized.

Some churches pour water as a picture of the pouring out of the Holy Spirit (Acts 2:17, 33; 10:45-48) while others sprinkle to symbolize the sprinkling of Christ's blood to wash away our sin (Heb. 9:19-22, 10:22, 12:24; 1 Pet. 1:2). Although our own church does not use these other methods, **they are acceptable for true believers.**

Does baptism save you from your sins?

Water baptism does not save anyone; union with Jesus does. In 1 Peter 3:21 the Apostle Peter says, *'Baptism... now saves you, not as a removal of dirt from the body but as an appeal to God for a good conscience, through the resurrection of Jesus Christ.'* Peter explains that external washing in water has no effect on one's standing with God. Rather, what saves you is an appeal to God that you trust in the resurrected Jesus to forgive your sins.

Should infants be baptized?

Some Christian traditions sprinkle, pour, or even immerse infants to show that their child will be raised in accordance with the gospel. While this is well intended, Jesus commanded the church to baptize 'disciples,' not potential disciples (Matt. 28:19).

Baptism is for those who have been circumcised in heart (Col. 2:10-12) and repented and believed in Jesus (Acts 2:38).

Because infants cannot consciously trust in Christ, Baptist churches believe they should not be given the sign of the New Covenant. If you were 'baptized' as an infant, we would encourage you to be baptized as a believer. This would not be a 'rebaptism,' but a true baptism. Presbyterian churches, on the other hand, practice infant baptism as they believe the new covenant promise extends to children of Christian parents and that the sign is rightfully applied to them. Once a child is baptized there is no need for a second baptism should he or she come to faith in Christ.

Can I ask people to come and see my baptism?

Yes! Baptisms are a perfect opportunity to invite unbelieving friends, family members, and co-workers to hear how Jesus has changed your life and can change theirs as well.

STOP

Did you learn anything new about baptism in this study? If so, what stood out to you?

Why do you think being baptized into a local church is important for a believer?

BRIAN

After his conversation with Dave, Brian was ready to be baptized. But he had questions about the Lord's Supper. Dave had encouraged him to wait a while before taking it. But Brian desired to join the church in taking the meal, so he asked to learn more.

THE LORD'S SUPPER

'As often as you eat this bread and drink the cup, you proclaim the Lord's death until He comes.' (1 Cor. 11:26)

On the night Jesus was betrayed, He shared the Passover meal with His disciples (Luke 22:14-23). This meal reminded Israel that God delivered them from slavery in Egypt by sacrificing an unblemished lamb and smearing its blood on the doorposts of their home. God promised that anyone who hid by faith under the blood of the Lamb would be spared from the judgment that was about to come.

God kept His word. Death fell on those who did not obey, and mercy fell on those who did. After the Passover, God miraculously led Israel through the Red Sea and on to the Promised Land.

Jesus' disciples did not realize that His impending death and resurrection would serve as a greater Passover to bring about their own exodus from sin (1 Cor. 5:7). As they sat, Jesus took bread, gave thanks for it, broke it, and handed it to the disciples saying, *'This is my body, which is given for you. Do this in remembrance of me'* (Luke 22:19). Afterward, He took a cup of wine and said, *'This cup that is poured out for you is the new covenant in my blood'* (Luke 22:19-20).

As He served those elements, Jesus instituted an ordinance that His church would observe until He returns and we celebrate with Him forevermore (Luke 22:18; Isa. 25). Today when the church gathers and shares in this ordinance, we 'proclaim the Lord's death until He comes' (1 Cor. 11:26).

 ILLUSTRATION

I'm wearing a wedding ring I received from my wife on our wedding day. After we exchanged vows, we exchanged rings as symbols of our love. The ring is not my marriage, nor did it create my marriage, but it does symbolize it. It says to everyone, 'This man is committed to his wife in a covenant of marriage.'

Similarly, the Lord's Supper doesn't create our relationship with Jesus. But it does represent the communion Christians share with Him. The bread and wine signify Jesus' body being broken and His blood being poured out for the forgiveness of our sins (Matt. 26:26-29).

Merely taking the elements doesn't impart anything to a believer other than a few calories. But when received by faith and in accordance with the Word, they serve as visible illustrations of gospel truth, which helps us to uniquely commune with Jesus.

In fact, the word 'communion' is often used to describe the Lord's Supper. This is appropriate because in the meal we renew our oath to follow Jesus and intend to commune with the Lord through faith and with other believers (1 Cor. 10:16-17, 11:17-22).

BRIAN

As Dave explained the Lord's Supper, Brian was amazed by the significance of the symbol Jesus left for His church. Brian then asked, 'Can you help me know whether it is okay for me to take the Supper or not?' Dave could tell Brian was burdened by not taking communion, so he tried to explain further.

The Lord's Supper should be served with both a *welcome* and a *warning*.

The Lord *welcomes* sinners to His table.

Jesus was the friend of sinners during His ministry and still is today (Matt. 11:19). The church does not serve the Lord's Supper to perfect people who have it together; sinners always fill His guest list. In light of this, we should '*welcome one another as Christ has welcomed you, for the glory of God*' (Rom. 15:7).

And yet, the church is also charged with guarding the Lord's Table.

This is done to honour God and protect people. As we'll see, the symbols of the meal point to something so significant that God will bring judgment on those who take it in an unworthy manner. Listen to the warning Paul gives the church at Corinth—

'When you come together as a church, I hear that there are divisions among you...it is not the Lord's Supper that you eat. For in eating, each one goes ahead with his own meal. One goes hungry, another gets drunk...do you despise the church of God and humiliate those who have nothing?... Shall I commend you in this? No, I will not... Whoever, therefore, eats the bread or drinks the cup of the Lord in an unworthy manner will be guilty concerning the body and blood of the Lord. Let a person examine himself, then, and so eat of the bread and drink of the cup. For anyone who eats and drinks without discerning the body eats and drinks judgment on himself. That is why many of you are weak and ill, and some have died' (1 Cor. 11:18-30).

Some among the Corinthian church had come to the Lord's Table in a way that led them to severe discipline.

People were holding onto their sin and taking the meal. This was a way of taking the Lord's name in vain, which brought judgment. As we search the Scriptures, we find four reasons someone should refrain from taking the meal so as to not take the Lord's Name in vain.

1. *The unconverted.* To not believe in Jesus, and then take the meal makes a mockery of the body and blood of Jesus, which are represented in the elements.

2. *The unrepentant.* Those who profess faith in Christ, but are living in unaddressed, unrepentant sin. This too makes a mockery of Jesus who gave His all for us.

3. *The uncommitted.* Jesus publicly shed His blood to unite us to Himself, and we must publicly be baptized and united with other believers to take His meal. This reason will be a point of disagreement among believers, though it seems consistent

with the Scripture and church history that one must be a baptized church member before participating in the Supper.

4. *The unauthorized.* In most cases, any professing believer under some form of church discipline should first be reconciled to that church.

At our church, we tell people who fit into any of these categories that they are welcome into our homes to share in a meal and discuss how we can help them follow Jesus. But during the Lord's Supper, we ask them to reflect on their sin and seek repentance and reconciliation while the rest of us participate.

This may seem harsh, but Jesus uses the ordinances to draw clear lines that echo His Words, *'Whoever is not with me is against me'* (Matt. 12:30).

 ILLUSTRATION

One Sunday, a young lady named Addie visited our church. A friend had talked to her about God and encouraged her to visit. During the end of the service, the church celebrated the Lord's Supper. Before the elements were shared, the pastor explained who should share in the meal and who should not.

She later shared that it was that night, when the elements passed by her that she understood the gospel she had heard both from her friend and during the service. She saw visibly that her fellowship with God was broken and she was on the outside of His people. It was then and there she knew she wanted Jesus to bring her into His church.

BRIAN

Brian had no doubt that he desired to be baptized. He wanted to share in the Lord's Supper with the rest of his church. He knew he wasn't perfect, but he also knew Jesus had been perfect in his place. But just like with the topic of baptism, Brian had a few lingering questions for Dave.

How often should a church take the Supper?

Churches are permitted to make this decision based on their own convictions. Jesus did not tell us how frequent 'often' is when He gave His instructions (1 Cor. 11:26). Though there's freedom, churches who take it less than once a month should consider why they've chosen to do it so infrequently when it seems to have been a regular part of the early church's life (Acts 2:42-47).

Why do we use bread and wine?

These were the elements the Lord used during His meal with the disciples. There is freedom regarding what type of bread and grape drink a church can use.

Should Christians take the Supper apart from the local church?

Some believers choose to take the Lord's Supper at home with their family, while camping, in small groups, or at their wedding (as my wife and I did). However, the Lord's Supper is not given to individual Christians who can take it wherever they want to have a special moment with Jesus. The Supper is a family meal that's given to the whole church to partake of together as they keep each other accountable (1 Cor. 10:16-17).

MEMORY VERSE

'In him also you were circumcised with a circumcision made without hands, by putting off the body of the flesh, by the circumcision of Christ, having been buried with him in baptism, in which you were

also raised with him through faith in the powerful working of God, who raised him from the dead' (Col. 2:11-12).

or

'As often as you eat this bread and drink the cup, you proclaim the Lord's death until He comes.' (1 Cor. 11:26)

 SUMMARY

As we've seen, baptism is not merely a religious dunking booth— nor is the Lord's Supper merely a snack before lunch. Jesus gave us these sacred signs to visibly mark out His people as the local church. They serve as sobering signs of celebration that point us to Jesus who died, rose, and now communes with His people by His Spirit.

WHAT'S THE POINT?

Church membership is committed love.

6. CHURCH MEMBERSHIP

BRIAN

The church was confusing for Brian, but not in a bad way. Every time he gathered with them on Sunday morning, he was baffled by their love for each other. On the surface, they didn't have much in common, but their love for Jesus and one another was evident.

As he and Dave talked, Brian described how God had grown his love for these people he never would have known apart from Christ. He remembered some of their first conversations about the church being a family, and he finally felt like he was beginning to understand what that meant.

Dave thought it was a good time to draw the connection between Brian's desire to be baptized and take the Lord's Supper with what it means to be a church member. Church membership wasn't something Brian had ever given much thought to, but he was ready to learn.

STOP

Why do you think someone should become a member of a local church?

How would that membership be different than membership in a country club or speciality store?

What reasons might someone have for not joining a church?

Commitment is an endangered species in our day. We like to keep our options open and preserve our freedom of choice. But God calls His people to think differently about their relationship with one another. Though the phrase 'church membership' doesn't show up in the Bible, the concept is nearly impossible to miss.

 'As in one body we have many members, and the members do not all have the same function, so we, though many, are one body in Christ, and individually members one of another' (Rom. 12:4-5).

When someone is spiritually baptized into Christ, they're united with the universal church. But when they're physically baptized in water, they're united to a local church that helps them live out their devotion to Jesus.

In case the terms are unfamiliar, the *universal church* refers to all people everywhere who have been born again and are spiritually united with Jesus. They're the redeemed from every tribe, tongue, and nation whose names are written in the Lamb's book of life. If you're a Christian, you are part of the universal church.

A *local church* is an assembly of specific Christians in a geographical area who are committed to gather regularly as worshippers and witnesses of Jesus. Whether it's the church in Antioch (Acts 13:1), Rome (Rom. 1:7), Corinth (1 Cor. 1:2), the churches in the region of Galatia (Gal. 1:2), or a church addressed in Revelation 2–3—the Bible consistently refers to the 'church' as a local assembly of believers. In fact, of the roughly 109 times the word 'church' is used in the New Testament, nearly all of them refer to a particular local church.

The New Testament doesn't recognize free-agent Christians who roam around uncommitted to a local church.

Baptism and the Lord's Supper are intended to give shape to a church's membership; they're intended only for believers, for those whose lives offer evidence of saving faith. This is why church membership should only be extended to those who are born again. It does no one any good to blur the lines between those who have a right standing with God and those who don't. While we should always be welcoming to all people, the names on a church's membership roll should, as best as humanly possible, reflect the names in the Lamb's Book of Life (Rev. 13:8).

While all Christians are members of the universal church, it's clear from Scripture that Christians are assumed to be committed members of local churches as well. To say it bluntly, if you're not joined to a local church, you're going to have a very difficult time obeying Jesus.

BRIAN

'Hold on,' Brian interrupted. 'Are you telling me that if I don't join our church, I'm not a Christian?' Dave leaned back, 'Brian, that's not what I am saying. But what I am saying is that whether you call it membership, partnership, or committed love, you are going to have a very tough time obeying Jesus apart from His church.'

Dave explained, 'Church membership helps to clarify how we obey many of God's commandments. He has designed us to follow Christ in a committed community. How about we look at some examples of this from the Bible?'

STOP

What do you think about the statement 'you are going to have a hard time obeying Jesus apart from the church'?
How do you think a local church helps you obey Jesus?
How could you help others in the church obey Jesus?

HOW DOES GOD USE CHURCH MEMBERSHIP TO HELP YOU OBEY HIM?

When most people think of membership, they think of joining Costco or country clubs for pleasure and enjoyment. But that's not what we mean when we talk about church membership.

Church membership is a way to describe the kind of relationship God calls believers to have with one another to

honour Him,

fulfil the Great Commission (ch. 9),

and help each other make it home to heaven.

Here are four characteristics of the relational flavour of church membership.

1. Voluntary.

Christians should willingly obey God's call to unite with other believers in membership. We do this not because of dutiful coercion, but out of faith that God's design is wise and good.

I recently spoke with someone who left another church for good but difficult reasons. He confessed that the only reason he joined our church was because he knew God commanded it. He said God used that act of faith-driven obedience to help him grow and heal in ways he never could apart from the church.

2. Intentional.

Love and unity do not just *happen*. They must be intentionally pursued and cultivated. Christians join a local church with the intent of developing relationships in which believers strive to do spiritual good to one another. We strive to help each other grow in Christ-like holiness.

3. Accountable.

Through church membership we develop what I like to call intentionally intrusive relationships. This doesn't mean that everyone is in everyone's business, but it does mean that *someone* is in *your* business. We all need people who hold us accountable to how we use our words, money, and time. We need people to challenge us when we sin and encourage us when we're struggling. The church is a family that does all we can to help each other honour Jesus publicly and privately.

4. Committed.

When a husband and wife get married, they commit to loving each other in tough and sweet seasons. Church membership is similar. Our love for one another will be tested. We will let each other down. We will sin against one another. Our preferences will not always be served. But church membership is a way of saying we intend, by the grace of God, to be responsible for each other. We will not be casual or occasional in our love. We are in this together until God shows us Scriptural reasons to join another local church.

BRIAN

The love Dave described in church membership was eye-opening for Brian. It didn't sound like the stale, legalistic commitment he'd envisioned. Instead, it sounded a lot like the way Jesus had loved him. This made him want to learn more about what the Bible said regarding membership.

1. MEMBERSHIP STRENGTHENS ASSURANCE

A Christian's assurance of salvation rests fully upon the finished work of Jesus Christ and the testimony of the Holy Spirit (Rom. 8:16; 1 John 4:13-18, 5:6-13). Membership in a local church never replaces this, but it does serves as an echo chamber of this good news.

When a church hears someone's profession of faith in Christ, baptizes them into membership, and welcomes them to the Lord's Supper, they're giving that person assurance of their salvation. In essence, the church is saying, 'We've heard your testimony and seen the way Jesus has changed your life. We have every reason to believe you are a brother- or sister-in-Christ.'

A prerequisite for church membership is a credible profession of faith.

This is why congregations must remove their affirmation through church discipline when a member repeatedly refuses to repent of sin (Matt. 18:15-18, see chapter 8).

Certainly, some churches are sloppy with membership and give out assurance too quickly. Even the healthiest of churches will wrongly affirm people's profession. But God uses church membership as a means of strengthening true believers' assurance of faith.

2. MEMBERSHIP CLARIFIES WHO WE GATHER WITH

Christians are free to enjoy time with anyone they desire. And yet, we must have a certain group of believers that we gather with regularly to carry out God's commands.

'Let us hold fast the confession of our hope without wavering, for he who promised is faithful. And let us consider how to stir up one another to love and good works, not neglecting to meet together, as is the habit of some, but encouraging one another, and all the more as you see the Day drawing near' (Heb. 10:23-25).

If you are looking for a verse that commands you to gather with the church, here it is. When someone becomes a Christian, they're not called to an isolated life with Jesus on a spiritual island. We're called to regularly gather together. But who are we to 'not give up meeting together' with? Is he speaking of our relationship with *all* Christians?

No. He's speaking about a conscious commitment to a specific group of believers.

These are people who are devoted to each other, intentionally fighting sin together, suffering persecution together, and involved in each other's lives. Church membership clarifies who exactly we gather with regularly.

3. MEMBERSHIP CULTIVATES LOVE

When we read through the New Testament we find around 50 unique 'one another' commandments. These commands teach Christians how to—you guessed it!—interact with each other in a way that reflects the love of God. We're to be kind to one another (1 Thess. 5:13), to carry each other's burdens (Gal. 6:2), to offer hospitality to one another (1 Pet. 4:9), to forgive one another (Eph. 4:32), and so on.

These descriptions of love assume a community with other believers. It's literally impossible to obey dozens of commands if you are not serving such a community. This includes the most basic command, for us to love one another.

'Just as I have loved you, you also are to love one another. By this all people will know that you are my disciples, if you have love for one another'– Jesus (John 13:34-35).

Love is the chief mark of the believer.

God is love, and therefore His children are to display His love through the power of His Spirit. A local church is to be a community marked by forgiveness because we've been forgiven much (Luke 7:47). We're to be marked by patience because Christ has been patient with us (Rom. 2:4; 2 Pet. 3:9). We're a people who serve and sacrifice because Christ has done so for us (John 13:1-17).

STOP

How has God shown His love to you? How should that same love be seen among believers?

Can you think of ways you have seen God's love put on display through His church?

God teaches us to love through diverse relationships. When local churches gather, it appears the members have little in common.

Our skin colours and our political tastes differ.

Our cultural backgrounds and economic situations vary.

We have distinct preferences and convictions.

This diversity can at times be challenging, but God uses it wonderfully. You see, when we're united with people who are different than us, we must stretch to love them, and they must stretch to love us. We must learn to listen, empathize, and be patient.

Despite our differences, what binds us together is our love for the Lord Jesus.

We each have unique testimonies, yet we all bear the marks of His divine love.

He died for us,

rose for us,

called us,

converted us,

and continues to hold us fast by His grace.

He has taught each of us what love is, and now, through committing ourselves to a local church, we commit to show this same love to others.

What happens when church members are committed to love one another? The church becomes a distinct gospel witness—one that looks different to the world. It's *through* our gospel-centred life together that hope is offered to the world. Membership, then, helps to clarify both who we love and how we are to love them.

4. MEMBERSHIP CLARIFIES WHO WE CARE FOR

Christians should do good to all people generally (1 Thess. 5:15) and other believers especially (Gal. 6:10).

> **And yet, the New Testament prioritizes caring for those in your local church.**

In fact, nearly all biblical references about 'caring for the poor' are descriptions of how believers tended for members of their community.

'So then, as we have opportunity, let us do good to everyone, and especially to those who are of the household of faith.' (Gal. 6:10)

 ILLUSTRATION

I've been blessed with many friends and acquaintances. We know people through church, our kids' sports leagues, and other community events. As we've developed relationships with these people, many needs have come to light. There are financial struggles, health conditions, and countless other plights.

While I'm concerned about each of those families and their needs, I only have a limited amount of time, energy, and resources. This forces me to make decisions about whom I can help and how much I can help them.

Out of all those who have needs, who should get most of my attention? My own family. My wife and children must be first and foremost. Certainly, our family sacrifices to help others, but my first responsibility is for them. This same should be true among Christians in the ways they relate to other church members.

Just as caring for the needs of our natural family isn't optional (1 Tim. 5:8), neither is caring for the members of our local church. On the last day, we'll be judged for how we served our brothers and sisters in need (Matt. 25:31-46; Acts 6:1-6). Withholding generosity is a serious sin because it forgets the generosity Jesus has shown to us (James 2:14-17; 1 John 3:16-18).

While we should always desire to be generous to one another, we must not enable those who are unwilling to care for themselves (2 Thess. 3:10-15). Knowing needs and discerning boundaries is greatly helped by church membership. One of the clearest examples of this is found in 1 Tim. 5:1-16, where Paul instructs Timothy about how the Ephesian church should care for widows among them. The church is to make a list of widows and to evaluate their needs based on certain criteria. He assumes the congregation knows these sisters well enough to evaluate their character and serve their needs. Church membership provides a necessary structure to help identify the needs of the flock.

STOP

How do you think a system of membership could help promote love and service?

Can you think of any ways membership could stifle that love?

One lingering question you might have is how meaningful membership works in larger churches. As a church grows to the point where members aren't able to know everyone, the leadership must adapt to ensure their church doesn't enable members to remain anonymous and unaccountable. Having a plurality of elders and planting new churches are among the options to avoid this. It also helps pastors serve with a clear conscience, knowing that none of Jesus' sheep are left unaccounted for.

5. MEMBERSHIP IS ESSENTIAL FOR PASTORS TO BE FAITHFUL

'Obey your leaders and submit to them, for they are keeping watch over your souls, as those who will have to give an account. Let them do this with joy and not with groaning, for that would be of no advantage to you' (Heb. 13:17).

 ILLUSTRATION

Shortly after becoming a Christian, I pastored a church plant. We intentionally started our church without membership. We wanted to be loving, but not legalistic. We knew the Bible had commands for us, but we saw no reason to formalize friendships and draw boundaries around relationships.

While our intentions were good, this move hindered our spiritual growth. We never really knew who 'we' were. There was genuine love, but as we grew, the lack of clarity regarding who was among us hindered discipleship, service, and unity. Guarding the Lord's Table was always hindered and our first attempt at church discipline was a disaster (see chapter 8 for more on discipline).

But one of the most revolutionary moments in my ministry came when I read that pastors *'are keeping watch over your souls, as those who will have to give an account.'* God says that on the Day of Judgment pastors will give an account to Him for the way they cared for the people He entrusted to them.

Pastors aren't responsible for every Christian everywhere in exactly the same ways. Rather, there are particular Christians who, through membership, have committed to submit to and obey them in the Lord. This assumes at the very least that these leaders know the people they're supposed to watch over.

Certainly, a pastor should care for anyone who visits their church, but they're not responsible for that visitor in the same way they are for a church member. Members are trusting and following and submitting to them because God has placed those pastors over them.

With this sort of responsibility entrusted to them from God, the church's leadership must know whom they will be giving an account for one day. Church membership makes this very clear.

STOP

Can you see how church membership serves a pastor's ability to care for the church?

How might a church's leadership struggle if the church's membership is not clearly defined?

How might a church's members be helped by having clearly identified leaders?

---

6. MEMBERSHIP CLARIFIES WHO CHRISTIANS LEARN FROM

Each member should be able to learn from another member (Rom. 15:14). The Holy Spirit gives every believer the ability to understand and apply God's Word to one another. While this is the case, God also supplies leaders in every congregation to oversee and equip members.

The Lord calls members to 'obey and submit' to the pastors of their local church. While submitting to leaders can be unnerving to some, it's actually a great grace to the flock. We will take up more about the relationship between leaders and the congregation in chapter 7, but let's consider one part of the discussion now.

In Hebrews 13:17 we saw a clear expectation that particular church members make a conscious decision to submit to and obey particular pastoral leaders. *How can a Christian submit to their leaders if they don't literally belong to a local church?* They aren't commanded to submit to *some* leaders or *all* leaders, but specifically to '*your* leaders.'

Church membership simply makes clear who the leaders are and what responsibilities the congregation has toward them.

This means the congregation has the responsibility to pick its leaders wisely; this means these leaders must care for the flock sacrificially. Membership helps Christians recognize and understand how to relate with the shepherds God has given to lead, feed, and protect their church.

7. MEMBERSHIP FOSTERS FRUITFULNESS

In the verses we just read from Hebrews 10:24-25 we are exhorted to '*consider how we may spur one another on toward love and good deeds...[and to]...encourage one another.*' Church members are commanded to think about, pray about, and intentionally find ways to cultivate good fruit in each other's lives.

These verses paint the picture of Christians who know each other well enough to give specific encouragements to foster fruitfulness. They know which promises to apply to one another's souls. These aren't casual acquaintances. These are people who know Jesus is coming soon and so they're committed to help each other be fruitful and faithful. You can't do that with every believer or just any believer you come across.

Church membership helps Christians focus their ministry on a particular group of fellow believers whom the Lord has brought together.

ILLUSTRATION

My mother had a garden when I was younger. I remember watching her till soil and plant seeds. I held the hose as water soaked the ground at the base of the plants. I remember mending the fence because my mom said it kept the hungry varmints at bay. We had to be relentless at pulling weeds—and when plants sprouted, we pruned and picked them. For the garden to be as fruitful as possible, we constantly tended it.

Church membership is a lot like gardening. We sow seeds of truth into each other's lives and water it with encouragement so that as much fruit as possible can spring up for God's glory. That kind of love doesn't happen through casual commitment. It comes through intentional, committed, and long-lasting relationship.

8. MEMBERSHIP HELPS US FIGHT SIN AND PERSEVERE IN FAITH

There's a line in a well-known hymn that confesses, '*Prone to wander, Lord, I feel it, Prone to leave the God I love.*' Our hearts are fickle. We struggle to fight sin's temptations and at times venture into compromise. This is true both of pastors and brand-new believers. Thankfully, God has given us the local church to help in our fight against sin's deceitfulness.

'*Take care, brothers, lest there be in any of you an evil, unbelieving heart, leading you to fall away from the living God. But exhort one another every day, as long as it is called "today," that none of you may be hardened by the deceitfulness of sin. For we have come to share in Christ, if indeed we hold our original confidence firm to the end*' (Heb. 3:12-14).

Satan is known as the tempter.

His delight is to deceive believers with sinful offerings that lead them to stray from God.

He assures us we can handle temptation.

He ensures us we could stop giving into a particular sin at any time.

Then, once we've given in, he attacks with shameful guilt. He convinces us we must conceal our sin so that no one will know.

The war against sin must not be fought alone. Instead, we are to exhort 'one another every day as long as it is called today.' *Who do you have that kind of relationship with?* Can you do that with all Christians everywhere? No. This is a command that can only be implemented among believers you regularly see. How else could we be held accountable? Membership crystalizes both whom we're committed to encourage and who is committed to encouraging us.

Does this mean we never help other Christians? No, of course not. But while Christians should seek to help and encourage all Christians when they're able, their primary responsibility is toward the people they've committed to in their local church.

Sadly, believers do occasionally become deceived and ensnared in sin. What does God say should be done when this happens?

'If anyone among you wanders from the truth and someone brings him back, let him know that whoever brings back a sinner from his wandering will save his soul from death and will cover a multitude of sins' (James 5:19-20).

In these verses, we're called to rescue brothers and sisters who've strayed into sin. *What brothers and sisters in particular are we to rescue? All brothers and sisters everywhere?* I certainly think you should help if you know of a straying Christian who isn't a member of your church. But notice the emphasis of this passage 'if anyone *among you* wanders from the truth.' What does 'among you' imply? It implies that there is a particular community of believers who regularly assemble around the truth of the gospel.

So, what happens when one among you wanders into sin? Someone needs to go get them. Meaningful church membership models the love of Jesus who left the 99 to rescue the one who had wandered into sin.

BRIAN

After considering all that Dave shared with him about church membership, Brian was ready to commit to the church. His readiness even surprised himself because he had never been the religious type. But the more he read the Bible and the more he spent time with people from the church, he knew God would use the intentional love of other believers to help him walk with God. He also thought he might be a blessing to others as well.

MEMORY VERSE

'As in one body we have many members, and the members do not all have the same function, so we, though many, are one body in Christ, and individually members one of another' (Rom. 12:4-5).

SUMMARY

God uses the voluntary, intentional, accountable, and committed relationships of church membership to help us persevere in faith. It makes straying into sin more difficult because you have people who have committed to love you and come after you if you leave. But it also puts *you* in a position to care for others and help them persevere as well.

WHAT'S THE POINT?

Follow leaders who follow Jesus.

7. LEADERSHIP

 BRIAN

Brian had always been wary of authority. Perhaps it was because of his father's bullying or his run-ins with the police. Either way, the thought of meeting with Pastor Thomas felt uncomfortable.

Dave assured Brian that the pastor was a godly man who believed the things he preached. He explained that Pastor Thomas always met with people who desired to join the church and get baptized.

Their lunch began with small talk that turned to Thomas asking Brian what God had recently been doing in his life. Brian shared about his friend's death and the way Jesus used that to show him his need for a Saviour. He explained that Dave had befriended him on his first day at church and that he had been growing in his faith ever since.

After a little while Pastor Thomas asked Brian, 'So do you have any questions for me?' 'I do', he replied. 'I see you up front on Sunday telling us about God, but can you help me understand what a pastor is and how you lead the church?'

STOP

Do you think of those in authority as being inherently enriching or inherently oppressive?

When you think about leadership in a church, what comes to mind?

Have you seen or heard of poor church leadership? If so, can you give an example?

Have you witnessed positive examples of leadership in the church?

A WORD ON AUTHORITY

There's something about authority that most of us dislike. We don't care to have someone over us telling us what to do. Because of this, many view resisting authority as a great virtue. But we should be cautious when we feel resistance well up in our hearts.

God is the great authority.

He has created a world in which authority and submission are as undeniable as gravity. Gravity is a gift because it keeps food on our plates and secures us from floating off into the atmosphere. Similarly, God's authority over us is a guarding, guiding gift that secures great blessing upon those who submit to it. He has given parents to teach, lead, and love as His reflection in the home (Exod. 20:12). He has designed police and government officials to protect citizens and ensure that evil does not overtake them (Rom. 13:1-7).

But something has gone terribly wrong in God's world.

Adam and Eve rejected God's rule over them, bringing corruption to the entire system. Now, those *in* authority are tempted to oppress and control those under their care, while those *under* authority are tempted to resist and dismiss guidance from those placed over them.

Navigating this maze can be disorienting. As Christians, we must not blindly get caught up in the revolt. There certainly are times to resist wicked authorities; but just as driving a car with no brakes is dangerous, we need the controlling structures God has given to us.

Godly leadership is a great gift to the world and the church. Godly leadership reflects the sacrificial servanthood of Christ. It uses power to protect and influence to edify. Its direction is toward our joy, not away from it. This should produce deep humility in the hearts of leaders, and great hopefulness in those who are being led.

King David's final words captured God's design for godly leadership, '*When one rules justly over men, ruling in the fear of God, he dawns on them like the morning light, like the sun shining forth on a cloudless morning, like rain that makes grass to sprout from the earth*' (2 Sam. 23:3-4). This benevolent vision provides the backdrop for our discussion of leadership in the church.

BRIAN

When Brian heard Pastor Thomas explain authority, he was shocked. He'd never thought of authority as good, let alone life-giving. His impression of church leaders had almost always been negative. He assumed they were just on power trips or trying to get into people's pocketbooks. But this gave him hope and he was interested to learn more.

LEADERSHIP IN THE LOCAL CHURCH

The Lord has designed the local church to operate in a way that promotes humility, service, and accountablity.

Jesus
'*Christ is the head of the church, his body, and is himself its Saviour*' (Eph. 5:23).

Any discussion about church leadership must begin with Jesus.

Jesus is the Saviour and Lord who is building His church (Matt. 16:18). God the Father *'put all things under his feet and gave him as head over all things to the church, which is his body, the fullness of him who fills all in all'* (Eph. 1:22-23). Jesus serves as the *'apostle and high priest'* who builds and intercedes for His beloved bride (Heb. 3:1).

Jesus said of His relationship with the church, *'I am the good shepherd. I know my own and my own know me…. I lay down my life for the sheep…. My sheep hear my voice, and I know them, and they follow me. I give them eternal life, and they will never perish, and no one will snatch them out of my hand'* (John 10:14-28). **Jesus serves as the chief Shepherd and Overseer of our souls (1 Pet. 2:25, 5:4).**

We begin our discussion about church leadership with Jesus because we're so prone to forget Him. While there's nothing inherently wrong with referring to a local church as 'my church' and as a human pastor as 'my pastor,' we must never forget that it is always Jesus' church and that any human who has authority in His church is merely a steward and 'under-shepherd' (1 Pet. 5:1-4).

STOP

How do you think congregations could be helped by regularly reflecting on Jesus as the chief shepherd?

What encouragement do you find in knowing that Jesus is your chief shepherd who is overseeing everything that happens in the church?

The Congregation

Jesus has given local churches both the charge and authorization over everything that happens in their midst (Matt. 16:19,

18:18-20). The congregation has the responsibility to oversee doctrine, discipline, membership, and stewardship.

In the book of Galatians, Paul rebukes the Galatian churches for being led astray into false doctrine (Gal. 1:1-10, 3:1). In John's epistles, he says that supporting faithful ministers causes a church to share in their faithfulness (3 John 8) while supporting false teachers causes them to share in their guilt (2 John 10-11). Furthermore, Jesus calls the gathered church to ensure unrepentant sin is addressed in ways that preserve purity (Matt. 18:15-17; 1 Cor. 5:1-13).

In the book of Revelation 2–3, we witness Jesus walking among churches, examining whether or not they've been faithful to Him. While leaders play an important role in the life of a church, in the end the congregation as a whole bears the responsibility of faithfulness.

STOP

Do you think most churches feel the weight of responsibility Jesus entrusts to them?

How could this congregational responsibility positively affect the culture of a church?

What dangers could come if a church was not careful to ensure that its members were Christians? How could non-believers with this authority negatively affect the church?

Elders and Pastors

One of the ways a church uses its authority well is by selecting godly leaders to lead them in obedience to Jesus. These leaders are called elders or pastors or bishops (Acts 20:28; Eph. 4:11; 1 Pet. 5:2). Congregations are responsible to recognize these leaders as gifts to the church. Leaders responsible to lead the church into spiritual maturity (1 Tim. 5:17), faithfully feed the church from His Word (2 Tim. 4:1-5), equip the church for the work of ministry (Eph. 4:11-16), and protect the church from false teachers (Titus 1:9).

'Pay careful attention to yourselves and to all the flock, in which the Holy Spirit has made you overseers, to care for the church of God, which he obtained with his own blood' (Acts 20:28).

In this verse we see God the Father, Son, and Holy Spirit working together on behalf of His church. Jesus the Son obtained the church by shedding His blood on the cross (Rev. 5:9). The Holy Spirit gifts and appoints elders to oversee and care for the church on the Father's behalf (1 Cor. 12:8-11). The church belongs to God, and He graciously cares for it by establishing leaders.

God tells us what to look for when selecting elders. They should be men with Christ-like qualities (1 Tim. 2:11–3:7; Titus 1:5-9). They should be 'above reproach,' which does not mean they're flawless, but that they're able to humbly care for the flock with a clear conscience and serve as an example of faith (1 Tim. 3:1-7; Heb. 13:7; 1 Pet. 5:1-5).

There are normally multiple elders at churches, because God intends numerous shepherds to work together to carry out ministry (Acts 11:30, 14:23, 15:22, 20:17; 1 Tim. 4:14, 5:17; Titus 1:5; 1 Pet. 5:1-5). A plurality of elders guards both the church and any single elder from having unchecked authority.

 ILLUSTRATION

Loving parents are a wonderful gift. A father who's tough and tender and a mother who's gentle and affectionate provide a caring combination that reflects God's love for His people. A home with parents like these is never free from problems but it has a stability and sweetness that God desires children to enjoy, honour, and obey (Eph. 6:1-3).

My wife didn't have a home like this growing up. Her mother was a wonderful woman, but her father was not a godly man. It has been a joy however to watch her find this sort of parental care from faithful pastors God has provided for her over the years.

Paul describes the care the Thessalonian church had received from Silas, Timothy, and him in this same way: *'We were gentle among you, like a nursing mother taking care of her own children. So, being affectionately desirous of you, we were ready to share with you not only the gospel of God but also our own selves, because you had become very dear to us.... For you know how, like a father with his children, we exhorted each one of you and encouraged you and charged you to walk in a manner worthy of God'* (1 Thess. 2:7-12).

BRIAN

As Pastor Thomas described the way leaders are supposed to love the church, Brian got quiet. Dave knew that family was a troubling subject for Brian. Brian's parents were anything but loving and whenever they came up in conversation, it was like salt in an open wound. Dave wondered if Brian heard what the pastor was saying or not.

Before Dave could say anything, Brian spoke up, 'My family isn't much like that. But I can see how God might be giving me a new kind of family here at the church. Dave and Ashley have been very kind to me, and so far, the leadership at the church has seemed a lot like what you are describing.'

Pastor Thomas told Brian he was encouraged to hear how God had challenged him and asked if he could share one of the most challenging passages for him as a pastor.

'Obey your leaders and submit to them, for they are keeping watch over your souls, as those who will have to give an account. Let them do

this with joy and not with groaning, for that would be of no advantage to you' (Heb. 13:17).

This verse captures the relationship between a congregation and the leaders who they have recognized as being gifted to shepherd them. The congregation is called to 'obey and submit' to the leaders. No, this doesn't mean elders control the lives of church members. What it does mean is that God expects members to have a general posture of submission as elders lead according to the Scriptures.

The church recognizes that God has entrusted the souls of the congregation to certain elders. Jesus is their Saviour, but one of the ways God helps His people persevere is through the help of godly leaders. This is why God charges pastors to *'keep a close watch on yourself and on the teaching. Persist in this, for by so doing you will save both yourself and your hearers'* (1 Tim. 4:16). God uses elders to help His people to heaven. They teach God's Word, warn of spiritual dangers, help ensnared sheep, and guide members to reconcile with one another.

As elders lead the flock, they do so knowing they 'will give an account' for the souls of their members. There is a day coming when all people will give an account for what they have done (Matt. 16:27; Rom. 14:12). Elders aren't exempt from this judgment. In fact, theirs will be more intense (James 3:1).

God is greatly angered by shepherds who oppress or neglect His flock, yet He promises to come among His sheep and shepherd them Himself (Jer. 23:1; Ezek. 34:1-31; John 10:1-30). After all, pastors are sheep whom the Lord has also called to serve as 'under-shepherds' in the ministry of Jesus the 'Chief shepherd' (1 Pet. 5:1-7).

As we get closer to that great day, pastors should prepare the church to be a pure bride for Jesus to receive. The Apostle Paul described ministry like this, '*I feel a divine jealousy for you, since I betrothed you to one husband, to present you as a pure virgin to Christ. But I am afraid that as the serpent deceived Eve by his cunning, your thoughts will be led astray from a sincere and pure devotion to Christ*' (2 Cor. 11:2-3). Satan is always lurking near, seeking to deceive and tempt and lure the flock away through trickery (1 Pet. 5:8). Pastors must do all they can to guard themselves and the flock from the tempter's attacks.

STOP

How has this description of what a pastor is and what a pastor does shaped your thinking about church leadership?

How ought this weighty calling to affect the members of a church?

At the end of Hebrews 13:17, the congregation receives an important reminder: '*let them do this with joy and not with groaning.*' As pastors strive to serve the church and prepare their people for heaven, the church should strive to make their pastors' ministry a joy. Pastors know ministry joys (1 Thess. 2:19-20; 3 John 4), but they also know its pains.

God commands church members to let their pastors serve with joy, not groaning.

It's easy to be provoked to 'groaning' when members get caught up in slander, grumbling, criticism, and gossip rather than humbly striving toward unity.

On the other hand, pastors are *encouraged* in their work when they see church members walking in obedience to God, trusting Him in adversity, enduring persecution, showing love toward one another, and generously giving for the sake of spreading the gospel (Phil. 1:3-5; 1 Thess. 1:2-3; 2 Thess. 1:3-4; 2 John 4). Churches should strive to honour God in all they do—including the ways they love their pastors.

> **STOP**
>
> What are ways you could encourage your pastors/elders in their labours?
>
> How would your encouragement help them to honour God?

> **BRIAN**
>
> Pastor Thomas asked Brian how he felt after hearing what the Scriptures said about elders/pastors. Brian admitted he had never thought about them giving an account to God for church members. 'I think I should pray for you more than I do,' Brian said.

Dave asked if Pastor Thomas could finish up their meeting by telling Brian about deacons and how they fit into the life of the church.

Deacons and Deaconesses

'*Whoever would be great among you must be your servant*' (Matt. 20:26).

While everyone in the church is called to serve, the Lord has designed the office of deacon for a unique kind of service. The word deacon literally means 'servant' which captures what the office is all about. Deacons are uniquely gifted members who oversee areas of practical ministry. Deacons carry out their ministry in co-operation with and under the oversight of the elders.

Elders and deacons were both active offices during the days of the apostles (Phil. 1:1). While their ministries are closely related, it's important to understand how they differ. Elders are responsible for spiritual leadership and instruction, while deacons work under the direction of the elders by caring for practical needs within the congregation.

Deacons first show up in Acts 6:1-7 when the apostles put forward godly servants to care for the needs of widows in the church. These servants oversaw the collection and distribution of resources to bring relief to suffering members. This fostered great joy and unity to the church, which are fruits of a deacon's service. This also freed the elders and apostles to focus their efforts on praying and explaining what the Scriptures teach about following Jesus, which resulted in the number of disciples growing greatly.

While it's important to maintain the distinctions between elders and deacons, we shouldn't assume elders do the 'real' spiritual work and deacons merely do physical work.

All service of the Lord Jesus is spiritual work, whether it comes in the form of words or works.

A church that doesn't faithfully preach the Word will have no heart, but a church with no good works has no hands. True words and compassionate works are both necessary for a church to be faithful (James 2:14-26). Elders and deacons labour together to ensure a church is being faithful in both areas.

Because of the importance of their role, deacons are to be 'dignified' in a way that allows them to be an example for the entire congregation (1 Tim. 3:8-13). Their qualifications are nearly identical to elders except they're not required to teach or exercise spiritual authority like elders. Deacons should be *full of the Spirit and of wisdom'* (Acts 6:3) because they are often placed on the frontlines of ministry where they need wisdom to appropriately care for people who are hurting.

As long as a church has a clear understanding of the difference between the role of elders and deacons, both men and women should be encouraged to serve in this capacity. Restrictions that forbid sisters from serving as pastors aren't in play because the office of deacon doesn't require exercising authority over men. Some churches disagree on this point, and it would be worth further study for you to make your own conclusion.

Exactly what deacons do is up to each individual church. Some deacons oversee the preparation of the ordinances, homebound members, mercy ministries for the poor, church finances, weddings, sound ministry, and many other things. Regardless of the tasks deacons are charged with, they should serve in faith knowing *'those who serve well as deacons gain a good standing for themselves and also great confidence in the faith that is in Christ Jesus'* (1 Tim. 3:13).

STOP

How might God use the role of a deacon to bring unity to a local church? What are some possible areas of ministry that are important, but should be handled by deacons so pastors are freed up to minister the Word more faithfully?

 BRIAN

After lunch, Brian and Dave thanked Pastor Thomas for spending the afternoon helping him learn more about leadership in the church. When he left, Dave asked Brian, 'So what did you think?' Brian was very encouraged, not only by the pastor's explanations, but by God's wisdom in organizing the church as He had. Brian knew he needed to keep growing in his own understanding of the Bible before he could serve in either of those capacities, but he desired to help in any ways he could.

MEMORY VERSE

'Obey your leaders and submit to them, for they are keeping watch over your souls, as those who will have to give an account. Let them do this with joy and not with groaning, for that would be of no advantage to you' (Heb. 13:17).

SUMMARY

God cares for His people by entrusting them to leaders who serve them in ways that honor God. Leaders must always imitate Jesus by using their authority to serve those under their care. We ought not to fear godly leaders, but trust God by following them as they follow God.

WHAT'S THE POINT?
Love cares enough to correct each other's sin.

8. CHURCH DISCIPLINE

BRIAN

Since Brian was ready to be baptized and join the church, he attended a membership class. During the class, Pastor Thomas briefly mentioned church discipline. Brian was confused because he thought the church wanted people to get involved, but church discipline seemed unloving and judgmental.

Dave joined Brian during the class, so afterwards they had coffee to process what he had heard. Brian brought up church discipline and suggested that Dave should help him see what the Bible said about it.

ILLUSTRATION

A number of years ago, a sobering ad ran during the Super Bowl. It was a black and white commercial that began by showing a girl standing on something, looking down. The sound moved from muffled to clear and was accompanied with the sound of splashing water.

After a few moments the camera angle moved behind the girl and showed her staring down into the water. Finally, the angle moved above the scene revealing the girl was on a dock, staring down into the water watching someone drown. The screen faded to a black screen and a voice said, 'If your friend was drowning, would you do nothing about it?'

The commercial was intended to challenge people to intervene in the lives of friends consumed by drugs. It was a call to stop watching them destroy their lives, and to do whatever was necessary to rescue them. The ad pushed people to be courageous with drug-addicted friends. It also provides a perfect picture of the heart behind church discipline.

 'Brothers, if anyone among you wanders from the truth and someone brings him back, let him know that whoever brings back a sinner from his wandering will save his soul from death and will cover a multitude of sins' (James 5:19-20).

> God intends church members to not allow one another to be consumed by sin.

> They should be compelled by grace to do whatever they can to rescue wandering brothers and sisters.

Just as helping someone addicted to drugs requires divine wisdom, we need God's wisdom to pursue wandering sheep *and* wisdom to know when to stop pursuing them.

STOP

If you were drowning, would you want someone to do whatever it took to rescue you?
What if you were drowning in a sin that would destroy your soul? Would you desire someone to rescue you?
If you saw a professing Christian make destructive decisions, would you feel the responsibility to intervene?

As we've seen throughout our study, the church's love should mirror the love they've received from God. Because of this, let's begin our study of church discipline by considering God's loving discipline toward His children.

'The Lord disciplines the one he loves, and chastises every son whom he receives' (Heb. 12:6).

God is the Father of all believers. We all were once far off in our sin, but He brought us near through the blood of Christ (Eph. 2:13). We have been reconciled as His beloved children and are being conformed into the image of Jesus (Rom. 8:29; Col. 3:10).

God uses many things to shape His people, including pain. This isn't popular, but God uses painful circumstances to break, shape, and transform us. God rarely brings spiritual growth in our lives through comfortable means.

Just listen to the way the author of Hebrews describes God's disciplining love:

'Consider him who endured from sinners such hostility against himself, so that you may not grow weary or fainthearted. In your struggle against sin...have you forgotten the exhortation that addresses you as sons? "My son, do not regard lightly the discipline of the Lord, nor be weary when reproved by him. For the Lord disciplines the one he loves, and chastises every son whom he receives." It is for discipline that you have to endure. God is treating you as sons. For what son is there whom his father does not discipline? If you are left without discipline, in which all have participated, then you are illegitimate children and not sons.... He disciplines us for our good, that we may share his holiness. For the moment all discipline seems painful rather than pleasant, but later it yields the peaceful fruit of righteousness to those who have been trained by it' (Heb. 12:3-11).

STOP

Have you seen God use painful circumstances in your life to draw you close to Him?

If so, can you share an example?

Did your earthly parents discipline you? If so, did it reflect the way God disciplines?

How has their discipline of you shaped the way you think of God's discipline?

 ILLUSTRATION

In 1501, a cathedral in Florence, Italy discarded a large piece of discoloured marble. It was scarred with scratches, chips, and missing chunks. After another well-known artist passed on the marble, a young struggling artist named Michelangelo offered to take it.

He built a shed around the 18-foot block of rock and spent night and day with it. For two years he used mallet, chisel, and drill on the block. Afterwards, he emerged and unveiled one of the most famous sculptures in history, a statue of a young King David.

When Michelangelo was asked, 'How did you get that sculpture out of that useless piece of marble?' he replied, 'I knocked off everything that wasn't David.' That's exactly what God is doing in your life right now if you are His child. He is using every means necessary to shape you and make you look like Jesus.

This is one role church discipline plays. One of the instruments God uses to shape us is the fellowship, exhortation, and discipline of the local church. I'm not talking about wicked churches abusing members or medieval torture chambers for the unfaithful.

I'm talking about God using loving, intentional relationships to help us fight sins that so easily entangle us. The local church is a place where everyone walks around with an 'under construction' sign on their chests. God uses the regular application of church discipline to help us grow in spiritual maturity, and to protect us from being consumed by sin.

STOP

What's one major reason people say they won't come to church?

I bet the answer to that question has something to do with '*all the hypocrites!*' I can't tell you how many times people have turned their noses up at the gospel because of the hypocrisy they've seen in professing Christians. This is one of the reasons God gives instructions about church discipline to local congregations.

WHAT IS CHURCH DISCIPLINE?

As we learned back in chapter 6, a *local church* is an assembly of Christians in a geographical area who are committed to gather regularly as worshippers and witnesses of Jesus. Membership is marked by committed, accountable, and encouraging relationships in the context of a local church.

Through church membership, Christians affirm one another's professions of faith and commit to helping each other live out their devotion to Jesus. When a church receives someone into membership, they make a statement to that person, to the church, and to the world.

To that person and to one another they essentially say, '*We affirm your profession of faith in Jesus and we're committing to love you, serve you, encourage you, and do all we can to help you to heaven— and we're expecting you to do the same for us.*'

At the same time, the congregation is saying to the world, '*This person is one of us. If you want to know who Jesus is, look at this person and listen to what they say. They will show you and teach you about Jesus.'*

But what happens when a professing believer begins to live in a way that contradicts their so-called faith in Jesus? The short answer is 'church discipline.' We're called to follow the process laid out in the New Testament that culminates in removing a professing Christian from church membership because they persist in unrepentant sin (Matt. 18:15-18; 1 Cor. 5:1-13; Titus 3:10).

When someone becomes a Christian, they don't stop sinning altogether, but their relationship with sin has utterly changed. We're now 'dead to sin' and 'alive to God' (Rom. 6:1-14). Because the Holy Spirit unites us to Jesus, we hate what He hates and love what He loves. True Christians fight against the sin that remains.

When someone who professes to follow Jesus persists in an unwillingness to fight their abiding sin, sirens should begin to sound.

That person is in danger of falling into destruction (Eph. 5:3-13; 1 Cor. 6:9-11). The church is in danger of being consumed with sin (1 Cor. 5:6; Gal. 5:9). The Name of Jesus is in danger of being blasphemed (Rom. 2:24).

When a member of a local church lives in unrepentant sin, and is unwilling to hear the pleas of other Christians to turn from their sin, they're living as a hypocrite. In this context, a hypocrite is someone who identifies as a Christian but lives without genuine repentance and devotion to Jesus.

This sin may be

persistent sexual sin (1 Cor. 5:1-11),

stirring up division in the church (Titus 3:10-11),

or continually disregarding clear Scriptural commands (2 Thess. 3:14-15).

When someone persists in this sort of lifestyle, there comes a time when a local church can no longer affirm his or her profession of faith. Because they are wilfully and stubbornly rejecting Jesus and His commands, we can no longer say to that person, *'We believe you are a Christian.'* We can no longer say to the world, *'This is what a Christian looks like.'*

This doesn't mean the church determines definitively whether or not someone is a Christian. The church doesn't have that kind of authority.

Only the Lord perfectly knows those who are His (2 Tim. 2:19).

This also doesn't mean the church punishes someone for their sin.

The Lord is the one who brings punishment for sin, either on Christ or on the final Day of Judgment (Rom. 12:17-21; 2 Cor. 5:19-21). Rather, the church serves as an instrument to *warn* unrepentant sinners of the coming judgment.

BRIAN

'Hang on!' Brian interjected. *'That sounds pretty judgmental! Didn't Jesus tell us not to judge other people?'* Dave turned the pages of his Bible and affirmed Brian's question.

Let's hear what Jesus says about judging others:

'Judge not, that you be not judged. For with the judgment you pronounce you will be judged, and with the measure you use it will be measured to you. Why do you see the speck that is in your brother's eye, but do not notice the log that is in your own eye? Or how can you

say to your brother, "Let me take the speck out of your eye," when there is the log in your own eye? You hypocrite, first take the log out of your own eye, and then you will see clearly to take the speck out of your brother's eye' (Matt. 7:1-5).

> **STOP**
>
> Does Jesus tell people to never judge other people?
> What does Jesus say we should do before we judge other people?
> Would someone be in a better place to judge others if they have first spent time examining their own sin? Why or why not?

Dave assured Brian that Jesus is *not* calling people to be judgmental toward each other when they're struggling with sin. Rather, Jesus' call to judge is rooted in love that aims to help straying sinners be rescued.

This is one of the tricky parts about church discipline. God uses a church full of fellow sinners as His instruments to rescue fellow sinners. This is why a church must have a community centred on the gospel. What I mean by that is the more a church is aware of their own need for Jesus' grace, the less room there will be for self-righteous judgmentalism.

Dave suggested they look at Matthew 18 together to see first-hand Jesus' teaching about how He desires His church to love straying members of His flock.

> **STOP**
>
> Take a few minutes to read all of Matthew chapter 18. Seriously, grab the Bible and read the chapter.

We'll wait right here for you.

Matthew 18 has one major idea that's captured in three major movements. The big idea of the chapter could be summarized like this: *God's people should be marked by a caring love that seeks those who stray and forgives those who repent.* This big idea is explained when Jesus describes the posture of the church (v. 1-14), a process in the church (v. 15-20), and then a picture for the church (v. 21-35).

POSTURE OF THE CHURCH

In verses 1-14, we see that Jesus' kingdom is marked by humility. Being one of His followers begins by humbly coming to Him like a child. This humility should inform the ways we treat one another.

The church must never become a source of stumbling. We should be neither harsh nor passive toward brothers and sisters while they're being consumed by sin. We must never look down on, think lightly of, or treat them with contempt. This could hinder them from repentance.

Rather, the church should reflect the heart of God. The LORD is like a shepherd who loves His sheep. If one of them strays away into danger, the shepherd will leave safety to go on a rescue mission to ensure that not even one is lost.

We must never be marked by arrogance or anger or apathy toward straying believers. Rather, we ought to be willing to risk comfort in order to rescue them. Jesus did this for us by leaving the glories of heaven to come to earth and rescue each member of the flock of God (Luke 19:10; Phil. 2:1-11). And thankfully, He never stops pursuing us in our sin.

Consider: *has God ever ceased loving and pursuing you despite all your wanderings?* Ask God to allow the love you have received from Christ warm your heart toward wandering sheep. Do not despise them, but seek, rescue, and reconcile them.

PURSUIT BY THE CHURCH

In verses 15-20 Jesus lays out a three-phase process that should guide the church when pursuing wandering sheep. Take a moment to reread it.

'If your brother sins against you, go and tell him his fault, between you and him alone. If he listens to you, you have gained your brother. But if he does not listen, take one or two others along with you, that every charge may be established by the evidence of two or three witnesses. If he refuses to listen to them, tell it to the church. And if he refuses to listen even to the church, let him be to you as a Gentile and a tax collector.' (Matt. 18:15-17).

Jesus gives the church a process to follow, though it doesn't replace the need for prayerful, wise, pastoral care. There are very few black-and-white, cut-and-dry situations. People are complex, and so are their struggles with sin. Churches must be careful not to allow the process to consume the posture Jesus commands us to have. Church discipline isn't merely an administrative process to put people back in place. It's a guideline for our love.

PHASE 1—PRIVATE

In verse 15 Jesus says, *'If your brother sins against you, go and tell him his fault, between you and him alone. If he listens to you, you have gained your brother.'* When someone sins, the first step isn't to gossip about it, post about it on social media, or ignore it. Rather, the person who has been sinned against, or who knows about the sin, should personally pursue the person who is in sin.

This sort of personal responsibility for one another is commanded in Hebrews 3:13: *'exhort one another every day, as long as it is called "today," that none of you may be hardened by the deceitfulness of sin.'*

> **STOP**
>
> Did you notice who has the responsibility to take the first step toward a sinning brother or sister?

You do.

I do.

It's our responsibility.

Personal responsibility to pursue others is spoken of elsewhere by Jesus (Matt. 5:23-24) as well as the apostle Paul (Rom. 12:18). Put simply, the peace and purity of the church are partially your responsibility. The spiritual health and growth of others is partly your responsibility. We *are* our brother's keeper.

The first phase or step of church discipline should be happening often in a healthy church. If I have a problem with another member, or know about something going on in their life that isn't good, I should feel the freedom and sometimes even the responsibility to have a personal conversation with them about it. When this happens, the church is, in a sense, always 'disciplining' one another.

We should be having these personal, intentional conversations to help each other fight sin, but also to point out evidences of grace, instruct each other with truth, and bear each other's burdens and sorrows.

The first phase of church discipline is both a normal and necessary part of following Jesus. And when it is happening regularly, it shows that later stages of discipline make a lot more sense.

> **STOP**
>
> Who has permission in your life to come to you if they see you in sin?
>
> Who loves you enough to speak words of correction?
>
> How do you receive words of correction? What makes it difficult?
>
> Do you love others in the same way?
>
> What makes this aspect of love most challenging?

Before we move to the second phase, we must notice the most important part of the first one. What's the aim of initiating a conversation with your brother or sister? Reconciliation. 'If he listens to you, you have gained your brother' (Matt. 18:15).

The word 'gain' means to win back. Church discipline, at every level, is about winning the souls of fellow church members back from sin. It's about their spiritual safety, the witness of the church, and the pleasure of God who is watching every bit of it.

This aspect of love is spiritual warfare. We're at war for people's souls. We must not allow them to drown in sin. Rather, God calls us to plead with people to be reconciled to Him (2 Cor. 5:18-20). We can be God's voice to straying sheep, and *we* can call them to see the Good Shepherd's love. This is a great honour and responsibility.

PHASE 2—PARTNER

Many times, people repent when they're confronted. They apologize; they ask for forgiveness. But unfortunately, not everyone does. Sometimes, they remain ensnared and unwilling. This is when we must get others involved.

'But if he does not listen, take one or two others along with you, that every charge may be established by the evidence of two or three witnesses' (Matt. 18:16).

If someone 'does not listen' it means they shut their ears to reproof and turn their heart away from being reconciled to God. Involving others often begins by getting a spiritual leader involved. Whether this is an elder or a small group leader, it's wise at this point to bring someone else into the conversation to confirm what's happening and provide spiritual wisdom (Prov. 11:14; Gal. 6:1-2).

Sometimes, this phase may be skipped because of unique cases of publicly scandalous sin (1 Cor. 5:1-13). Generally, however, the second phase can last a significant amount of time. Because repentance from sin is difficult to discern, a small group of believers will walk with the struggling sheep for quite a while to help them repent of whatever ensnared them. I've seen numerous pastoral situations reach this phase and been a witness to God miraculously working grace in people to free them. We should always pray for this result.

BRIAN

Brian could see that Jesus had given clear instructions to the church. He was encouraged to see how the church's love was supposed to model Christ's love for the church. Brian was eager, however, to learn what happens when someone does *not* receive correction, but rather chooses to keep going his own way.

PHASE 3—PUBLIC

At some point, when a person won't respond to the pleas of those close to them, the entire church must be involved. God uses the church as the final messenger of mercy to this wandering sheep. No one desires the process to get this far, but sadly at times it must.

'If he refuses to listen to them, tell it to the church. And if he refuses to listen even to the church, let him be to you as a Gentile and a tax collector' (Matt. 18:17).

Since the entire church is committed to caring for this person's soul, the entire church bears the weight of being a sort of ultimate warning before they stand before God.

In our church, this third phase belongs only to church members.

We don't have this sort of discussion during a regular worship service, but a meeting where only members are invited. During this time, we 'tell it to the church' by sharing as many details as necessary without tempting people to speculate or obtain unnecessary information.

When we 'tell it to the church' we encourage anyone who knows them personally to use their relational capital to persuade the individual to repent. For those who don't know this person, we usually encourage them to remain steadfast in prayer, but not attempt to build a relationship with them at that time. This counsel is not based on any sort of biblical command, but solely on what seems wise.

Those who are involved in the process must guard their hearts.

In Galatians, the Apostle Paul explains, '*If anyone is caught in any transgression, you who are spiritual should restore him in a spirit of gentleness. Keep watch on yourself, lest you too be tempted*' (Gal. 6:1-2). Those who try to restore wandering sheep can be tempted toward anger, complaining, and self-righteous judgmentalism. They must continually keep their eyes upon Jesus and pray for Him to guard them from sinful pride.

What happens if the wandering person doesn't repent?

Jesus says, '*If he refuses to listen even to the church, let him be to you as a Gentile and tax collector*' (Matt. 18:17). The Jesus who calls us to pursue wandering sheep is the same Jesus who tells us there comes a time to humbly judge others and remove our affirmation of their profession of faith.

This is the part of the process most people think of when they hear 'church discipline.' When a church reaches this part of the process, they formally renounce their affirmation of someone's profession of faith. This means they are no longer members of the church and no longer welcome to take part in the celebration of the Lord's Supper.

When Jesus commands the church to treat the unrepentant person *'as a Gentile and tax collector'* He doesn't mean they can't come to church anymore, He means they're no longer to be treated as a believer. Christians are still to love them—not as a brother, but the way Jesus loved sinners.

This decision by a congregation is heart-breaking.

It brings great sorrow. When a church makes it to this point, it's always hopeful that such an act will bring both the unrepentant person to restoration and the church as a whole to humility.

If someone is under church discipline, they're welcome to continue attending worship services.

In fact, there's no better place for a sinner to be than in a place where they can hear the clear proclamation of the gospel. But they shouldn't take the Lord's Supper, nor participate in the normal fellowship of the church (1 Cor. 5:11). This may of course be impossible in some cases, but generally, this should be the church's posture.

 ILLUSTRATION

A few years ago, a church was disciplining a long-time member for repeated drunkenness. The process had gone on for around two years and was very painful for the congregation. During the process one particular member pushed back on the recommendation to excommunicate the person.

A few of the pastors visited the sister who objected and during their conversation, she began to cry and confessed that she had not been living for God's pleasure. She said that the reason she was upset about the discipline of the man was because she realized that she was in the same condition. God used the faithful process of church discipline to put His glory on display and draw people to Himself.

PICTURE FOR THE CHURCH

How should the church treat someone who does finally repent? They should forgive that person and receive them back into the fellowship of the church. Forgiveness is challenging for all of us, the Apostle Peter not excepted: *"'Lord, how often will my brother sin against me, and I forgive him? As many as seven times?" Jesus said to him, "I do not say to you seven times, but seventy-seven times."* (Matt. 18:21-22).

> **Jesus didn't mean to keep a tab and then after 77 times cease forgiving.**

He was teaching them and us that as the Lord has forgiven us, so we ought to forgive those who struggle in sin yet seek to be reconciled.

The parable of the forgiving King that follows this instruction paints a vivid picture of our responsibility as forgiven people to forgive those who seek restoration. Again, the goal of church discipline is never punitive.

> **It's *always* restoration and reconciliation.**

STOP

What could make extending forgiveness to someone difficult?
How could reflecting upon Jesus' forgiveness help you to forgive someone else?

What testimony would a church have if it extended forgiveness to someone who had previously been excommunicated but had repented of their sins?

How might people outside the church misunderstand church discipline? How should that affect the way we follow Jesus' commands?

 ILLUSTRATION

To conclude, I'd like to share with you the testimony of my friend Michael. He was excommunicated from his local church for persistent unrepentant sexual immorality and lying.

Years later, God used his church's faithful act of tough love to change his life. Here's a letter he read to that same congregation seven years after he was formally disciplined:

'It's very hard to articulate the feelings I have when I consider God's kindness to me as expressed through the love of this church. When I walked away from this church and from God, my life was marked by deception, hypocrisy, and immorality. I lied to you all with my life if not my words. For that I am very sorry. I brought shame to my parents, my family, and most bitterly, to my Lord. But in the face of my wandering, God saved me from my sin and brought me to repentance...

I want to commend to you the men that make up your pastoral staff. They obeyed Scripture when it was not easy to do so. Matthew 18 gives the guidelines for church discipline and they followed them.

They also did what they did not have to do. They didn't have to treat me the way they did during the process. They didn't have to call me and ask how I was doing. Get coffee together. Encourage me. Tell me they were praying for me. Email me devotionals. They didn't have to appeal and appeal and appeal to me that I would turn and repent. I would have expected, or at least, understood a desire to dismiss me quickly and quietly. But instead, they demonstrated amazing love to me. I was removed from membership for my own sake, yes. But, mostly, it was for you and for the reputation of the Gospel.

Apart from the weekly proclamation of the gospel and careful expositing of God's Word, I believe there are few if any ordinances of the church that bring the gospel more to bear than the proper practice of church discipline. I hope you are as encouraged as I am when I read Hebrews 12. "For the Lord disciplines the one he loves." The one he loves!

You loved me by disciplining me. You helped me to see the severity and beauty of Christ's sacrifice... Because of church discipline I had my eyes opened... because of church discipline, I tasted the world and found it bitter... because of church discipline I felt the cold contrast of life outside the church. But I remembered something of fellowship, grace, and love. I remembered this church. The Lord used these pastors and your shining example to draw me back to Himself... I thank God for them. And I thank God for you.'

BRIAN

Brian was amazed at the way God used what many would consider harsh treatment as an act of love. Brian hoped that he would never need people to pursue him with that kind of love, but he was also hopeful that if he needed it, they would, just as Jesus had.

MEMORY VERSE

'Brothers, if anyone among you wanders from the truth and someone brings him back, let him know that whoever brings back a sinner from his wandering will save his soul from death and will cover a multitude of sins' (James 5:19-20).

SUMMARY

God shows His love for His people through the church. If we stray from God, He loves us by using the church to help us turn from our sin and come back to Him.

WHAT'S THE POINT?

Christians help each other follow Jesus.

9. WHAT IS THE MISSION OF THE CHURCH?

BRIAN

It had only been a few months since Brian first visited the church, but he knew he was not the same person he used to be. God had given him a new desire to serve Him and help others come to know Him. *But how should he do that? What was the church doing that he could be a part of?*

At his next breakfast with Dave, Brian explained what he was feeling. Dave reached for his Bible and began thumbing through the pages. As he did, he told Brian that the Holy Spirit was changing his heart to be devoted to the purpose God has for His church.

As he held open the Bible, he looked at Brian and said, 'What I'm about to share with you is what Jesus says His church is supposed to be doing while we wait for His return. This is what many call the Great Commission.'

'*All authority in heaven and on earth has been given to me. Go therefore and make disciples of all nations, baptizing them in the name of the Father and of the Son and of the Holy Spirit, teaching them to observe all that I have commanded you. And behold, I am with you always, to the end of the age*' (Matt. 28:18-20).

While there are many important things churches can do, there are only a few things they *must* do. The Great Commission is one of them. It serves as a mission statement for the church. It captures what Jesus wants His church to be doing until He returns. To unpack this Commission, let's consider Jesus' authority, Jesus' command, and Jesus' promise.

1. JESUS' AUTHORITY

As Jesus gave His final command to His disciples, He declared that all authority on heaven and earth had been entrusted to Him. That was a radical claim that must not be breezed over. The Gospels explain that Jesus is the ever-existing Son of God who left heaven to rescue us. He is God, yet He became man. As the Apostle John put it, *'The Word became flesh and dwelt among us'* (John 1:14).

Jesus lived a life free from sin.

He always pleased God the Father,

and proclaimed the good news of God's Kingdom.

He called people to repent of their sins and trust in Him.

He performed miracles to prove that He had authority to forgive people's sins.

But rather than being embraced as Lord, Jesus was betrayed, arrested, mocked, beaten, and tortured to death on a cross. After three days in the grave, however, God rolled back the stone to display that Jesus had risen from the dead! Jesus was alive! Jesus *is* alive! The victorious Son of God has defeated sin's curse of death.

Following His resurrection, Jesus appeared to hundreds of people over forty days. When He declared to His disciples that *'all authority in heaven and on earth has been given to me,'* He was claiming ultimate sovereignty. Many of His hearers would have recognized how this startling claim echoes the seventh chapter of Daniel's prophecy in which we see a heavenly courtroom assembled for the Day of Judgment:

'As I looked, thrones were set in place, and the Ancient of Days took his seat. His clothing was as white as snow; the hair of his head was white like wool. His throne was flaming with fire, and its wheels were all ablaze. A river of fire was flowing, coming out from before him. Thousands upon thousands attended him; ten thousand times ten thousand stood before him. The court was seated, and the books were opened...and there before me was one like a son of man, coming with the clouds of heaven. He approached the Ancient of Days and was led into his presence. He was given authority, glory and sovereign power; all peoples, nations and men of every language worshiped him. His dominion is an everlasting dominion that will not pass away, and his kingdom is one that will never be destroyed' (Dan. 7:9-14, NIV).

This sobering scene reminds us that a Day is coming when all people will be judged according to what they've done (Rom. 2:4-6; Matt. 16:27). On that day, there will be no more chances to repent. Those who have been forgiven by faith in Jesus will be received into His everlasting joy, but those who have not will be cast from His presence into everlasting torment (Matt. 25:46).

When Jesus says all authority in heaven and earth has been given to Him, He's claiming to be the King of kings and Lord of lords who will judge every person who ever lived.

This sobering reality lies before the church. Jesus demands that His church go into the world and call people to repent in preparation for the Day of Judgment. Because heaven and hell are real, the church must fulfil their calling with urgency and intentionality. This is the banner that hangs over everything to which the church gives its time, energy, and resources.

STOP

How does Jesus' authority to rule and judge all people affect the church's mission?

What sort of response should it produce in your life as an individual Christian?

BRIAN

Brian had never thought about the church in light of the Day of Judgment before. This gave fresh urgency and sobriety to him as he considered his many friends who didn't know Jesus yet. It also made him wonder how the church could work together to tell more people about who Jesus was and what He called them to do.

2. JESUS SAYS MAKE DISCIPLES

With the Day of Judgment in view, Jesus commands His disciples, 'Go therefore and make disciples of all nations.' A disciple is someone who has left everything to follow Jesus. Jesus says that as they await His return, His disciples are to make more disciples.

Jesus' call to discipleship is given with the same backdrop of the final Judgment:

'If anyone would come after me, he must deny himself and take up his cross daily and follow me. For whoever wants to save his life will lose it, but whoever loses his life for me will save it. What good is it for a man to gain the whole world, and yet lose or forfeit his soul? If anyone is ashamed of me and my words, the Son of Man will be ashamed of him when he comes in his glory and in the glory of the Father and of the holy angels' (Luke 9:23-26, NIV).

The daily lives of Jesus' disciples are to be marked by obedient submission to Him and dependence upon His grace until the day He returns for them.

Jesus' mission to 'make disciples' was clear in the mind of the early church.

Jesus sent the promised Holy Spirit to empower believers to serve as His witnesses (Acts 1:8). They risked their lives to take the Gospel from town to town to make disciples and establish new churches. The book of Acts and the New Testament letters do not make sense apart from the Great Commission.

The apostle Paul echoed Jesus' instructions by telling Timothy, *'what you have heard from me in the presence of many witnesses entrust to faithful men, who will be able to teach others also'* (2 Tim. 2:1-2). The church is responsible to

proclaim,

entrust,

and pass on the gospel to others

who will do the same. In short, the mission Jesus gave His church was to

be disciples

who make disciples

who make disciples.

BRIAN

It made sense to Brian that Jesus' church should dedicate their lives to help people know Him. But the Great Commission seemed overwhelming to him, so he asked Dave if he could help him understand exactly how they were supposed to go about making disciples. Dave paused for a minute and said, 'Okay, there are a few things that might be helpful here, let me try to explain.'

The Great Commission has two primary applications:

one among unbelievers,

the other among believers.

The work among unbelievers is called evangelism, while the work among other believers is called discipling.

1. The church evangelizes unbelievers by calling them to repent of their sins and believe in Jesus.

Evangelism is the first step in the disciple-making process. The church is called to proclaim the good news of Jesus' death and resurrection to the people God has placed around us. We call unbelievers to turn from their sin and believe in Jesus as Lord and Saviour. We call them not simply to make a decision about Jesus, but to become a disciple of Jesus.

'You are a chosen race, a royal priesthood, a holy nation, a people for his own possession, that you may proclaim the excellencies of him who called you out of darkness into his marvelous light' (1 Pet. 2:9).

Jesus rescued us from the darkness of our sin, and now He has given us the honour and responsibility of calling others to that same hope.

This seems like a good place to point out that Jesus' purpose for the church is to 'make disciples of all nations' (Matt. 28:19). The evangelistic efforts of churches should never be limited to just one ethnic group. Why? Because Jesus isn't just Lord over India or Africa or America or Antarctica—He is Lord over all people in every land.

Jesus died to save sinners from every nation and has commanded His church to make the good news known to them.

STOP

Who are some of the people God has placed in your life who do not yet know Him?

How can your local church help you reach them with the gospel?

How are you able to help other believers reach their unbelieving friends with the gospel?

How should Jesus' aim to save people from every people group impact your life?

How are you tempted to only associate with people who look like you or have similar cultural preferences?

How does love for Jesus and obedience to the Great Commission compel you to grow?

---

2. The church helps fellow believers faithfully follow Jesus.

Once someone becomes a believer, the work of being a disciple has only just begun. God is working to conform us to the image of Jesus (Rom. 8:29; Col. 3:10). While God uses everything in our lives to mature us, a central part of His work is done in and through the local church.

As we talked about in chapter 6, local churches should cultivate relationships in which believers aim to do spiritual good to one another. The leaders of local churches equip members to grow up into spiritual maturity that reflects the character of Jesus (Eph. 4:11-16). Central to these relationships is a love that helps each other obey all Jesus has called us to do (Matt. 28:20). The call to make disciples is not an elective option or a mission given only to the super spiritually mature. If someone is following Jesus, they ought to be helping others follow Him as well.

The way local churches aim to accomplish the Great Commission will vary from congregation to congregation. But in general, there should be a regular rhythm in which local churches gather together to build up believers and then scatter abroad to evangelize the world. There's certainly overlap in this work, but each part focuses on the mission of making disciples.

3. When the Church Gathers

'When you come together.... Let all things be done for building up' (1 Cor. 14:26).

For 2,000 years, believers around the world have gathered on Sunday mornings to worship the One true God through Jesus His Son. Though there's discussion about how Sundays ought be used, it's a day when believers stop our normal lives, assemble as the church, and expectantly feed on the Word of God together. As we do, we aim to build each other up in spiritual health.

Since we know it's God's Word that has power to convict, encourage, and equip us (2 Tim. 3:16-17), everything that happens in a healthy church's gathering will be centred on the Scriptures.

+ When we sing, we sing songs filled with Scriptural truths that instruct our minds and warm our affections (Eph. 5:19).

+ When we read portions of Scripture from both the Old and New Testaments, we feast upon His Word together (1 Tim. 4:13).

+ When we pray, we pray individual and corporate prayers that are shaped by what God's Word teaches us to value (1 Tim. 2:1-8).

+ When we preach, we proclaim messages saturated with gospel truths that exalt Jesus (2 Tim. 4:1-2).

+ When we celebrate baptism and the Lord's Supper, we see the Word portrayed in these living illustrations (Rom. 6:3-4; 1 Cor. 10:16).

God uses the week-in and week-out gathering of His people around His Word to make them more like Jesus.

But believers aren't the only people present when the church gathers. Very often, non-Christians will gather with the church. Many non-believers know they don't believe, while others are self-deceived. Either way, God uses the truth from His Word and the love of His people to convict them of the truth (1 Cor. 14:24-25).

Because of this, local churches should be sure to make the gospel clear in every service. Furthermore, church members should prayerfully be watching for opportunities to engage in conversation with visitors. Who knows what God is up to?

3. WHEN THE CHURCH SCATTERS

'Therefore, we are ambassadors for Christ, God making his appeal through us. We implore you on behalf of Christ, be reconciled to God' (2 Cor. 5:20).

An ambassador is an official representative of a country's government in a foreign land. Jesus is the authoritative King of heaven who has commissioned His disciples as His ambassadors. When a church gathers, it does so as a community of His representatives on earth. And when we scatter, we go out in His authority—calling people to *'be reconciled to God.'*

It's interesting that while the gathering of the church is of utmost importance, most of what God calls the church to do occurs when they scatter. As we go out together into our homes, communities, small groups, and beyond, we go as His representatives.

You'll remember from our discussion in chapter 2 that the early church spent time together daily (Acts 2:42-47). But as they did, they always had an eye toward evangelism. Acts 2:47 (NIV) tells us these first Christians were *'praising God and enjoying the favour of all the people. And the Lord added to their number daily those who were being saved.'*

With all God was doing on the *inside* of this church, you might think they were tempted to forget about those on the outside. But that couldn't be further from the truth. They loved each other and shared grace with each other, but their love was directed not just inward, but outward as well.

This church wasn't isolated in an ivory tower or secluded like an exclusive country club. Instead, they lived out the gospel *and* preached the gospel. Their learning and loving and worshipping fuelled the mission of making disciples among the lost. As a result, *'the Lord added to their number daily those who were being saved.'*

Evangelism wasn't happening at a once-a-week event or a once-a-month revival. It marked the daily life of the church. They were regularly praying for God to open doors for the Word and they courageously stepped through those doors to speak words of life (Col. 4:2-6).

Did you notice that *'the Lord added to their number'*? As the church aims to make disciples, we know that no one will be saved apart from God's word. As a pastor once said, 'Our job is to faithfully share the gospel in the power of the Holy Spirit and leave the results up to God.' This takes the pressure off us and frees us to rely fully on God to save His people.

This is precisely what happened in Acts 16 when Paul proclaimed the Gospel in Philippi. As he preached to a group gathered by the river, Luke tells us what happened: *'The Lord opened her [Lydia's] heart to pay attention to what was said by Paul'* (Acts 16:14b). God used the faithful preaching of the gospel to save Lydia from her sin. Afterward, she was baptized and her home became a meeting place for Christians (Acts 16:15, 40). In other words, a church was birthed in Philippi!

God worked in the early church to do both evangelism and what's commonly called missions.

> *'Missions'* **refers to the sending of Christians to plant churches in unreached areas or assist existing churches in those areas.**

While there are many important discussions about how evangelism and missions should be done, there can be no doubt that churches must be active in this work. In the words of John Piper, Christians have three possible responses to the Great Commission: 'go, send, or disobey.'[1] In light of the final judgment, churches have no right to sit on the sidelines and ignore the command of Jesus to 'make disciples among the nations.'

STOP

Are you prayerfully seeking opportunities to speak of Christ?
Are you actively having people who don't follow Christ in your home?
How does your church's praying, preaching, and teaching compel people to consider how they may take the gospel to those who have never heard of Jesus?

---

1   See John Piper, 'Driving Convictions Behind Foreign Missions', January 1, 1996. <https://www.desiringgod.org/articles/driving-convictions-behind-foreign-missions>. Accessed April 2019.

Before we go on, we need to take a moment to answer an important question about the church's role in blessing the community. Many churches today see the mission of the church as being a blessing to the community in which they live. They show Christ's love by feeding the hungry, clothing the poor, caring for orphans and widows, and many other things commanded in the Bible.

It's essential to distinguish between what the church *must* do and what individual Christians *ought* to do. To help us sort this out, let's evaluate this statement:

> **Christian churches must serve their communities by working for justice and helping the needy.**

What this must not mean is that a local church is required to have staff, budget lines, and programs dedicated to influencing political policies, having a food pantry, and offering tutoring programs to underprivileged youth. Jesus doesn't require this of His church.

But what it *does* mean is that members of local churches should be active in labouring for justice and putting the love of Christ on display in whatever arena God places them. We cannot ultimately transform the world, but we must distinctly put the light of God's truth and grace on display as we seek to make disciples among the nations.

 'In the same way, let your light shine before others, so that they may see your good works and give glory to your Father who is in heaven' (Matt. 5:16).

When we are *at home*, we do laundry, make meals, and seek to live out the gospel together.

When we're among *our neighbours*, we serve them, develop friendships with them, and prayerfully help them engage with Jesus' call to repent and believe.

At *work*, we labour honestly and diligently to be a blessing, earn a wage, and help our co-workers become followers of Jesus.

Among *the needy*, we ought to clothe and feed and serve them, even as we point them to Jesus who died for the sins of sinners like them—and like us.

> **STOP**
>
> Why is it important to make the mission of the church clear?
> What are other important things the church could do?
> How do these important things differ from what the church must do (make disciples)?

> **BRIAN**
>
> Brian had lots of questions about the church's role in serving the community, but he was thankful that Dave helped him to see the overarching importance of making disciples. He believed the Great Commission was God's purpose for believers and he was ready to get involved in any way he could.

4. JESUS PROMISES HIS PRESENCE

In Jesus' final words, we find one of the sweetest promises in all of Scripture: *'Surely I am with you always, to the very end of the age.'* Jesus assures us that He will not abandon us in the midst of the mission.

He promises that He will go with us.

This means that when you prayerfully invite your neighbour or co-worker over for dinner and share the gospel with them, He is with you. When you speak with your mother or father and tell them that Jesus is your Saviour and can be theirs as well, He is with you. When you talk to the people at your job about repenting from sin and trusting in Jesus, He is with you. When you suffer, when you're weary, when you're fearful, when you're persecuted—Jesus is with you *always*.

When we walk among wolves, their growls must not deter us, for our Good Shepherd is with us. He is our strength, our wisdom, and the one who empowers us to keep pressing on. In Hebrews 13:5-6 (NIV) God has said, *"'Never will I leave you; never will I forsake you.' So we say with confidence, 'The Lord is my helper; I will not be afraid. What can man do to me?'"*

We shouldn't be controlled by fear of people.

They may persecute us, but if Christ is with us, the worst thing they can do is kill us and send us to eternal glory to be with the One our heart longs to see (Matt. 10:28).

And did you notice how long He promises to be with us? *'Until the end of the age.'* Jesus promises to guide, guard, provide for, and protect His followers until the day we see His face. All of history is moving to a moment when Christ will return and take us to be with Him. What a day that will be! Lord, let it be today!

But until He comes, there is work to be done. So let us risk everything to *'go and make disciples of all nations.'*

BRIAN

As Dave explained the Great Commission, Brian began to smile. He knew God had used Dave, Ashley, and the rest of their local church to help him grow. There were certainly ups and downs along the way, but he knew the church's obedience to the Great Commission had changed his life and his eternal destiny.

Brian also knew God had given him friendships with many people who were far from Jesus. He began to pray that God would use him to reach others for Jesus. He met with his pastor who helped him learn how to share the Gospel and even took him to the park to talk with people about following Jesus.

As Brian's love for God grew, so did his desire to tell others about him. He shared Christ with friends, family, and even made plans to go on a mission trip to a place where there were few followers of Jesus. Brian was amazed that God was using him to reach others for Christ, but he knew that if God could save him, He could save anyone.

 MEMORY VERSE

'Go therefore and make disciples of all nations, baptizing them in the name of the Father and of the Son and of the Holy Spirit, teaching them to observe all that I have commanded you. And behold, I am with you always, to the end of the age' (Matt. 28:19-20).

 SUMMARY

God rescued us from our sin to know Him, but also to help others come to know Him. As we go into the world to proclaim His Gospel we go knowing that He is with us and will provide everything we need to do what He has called us to do.

IX 9Marks

This series of short workbooks, from the 9Marks series, are designed to help you think through some of life's big questions.

IX 9Marks

Building Healthy Churches

9Marks exists to equip church leaders with a biblical vision and practical resources for displaying God's glory to the nations through healthy churches.

To that end, we want to see churches characterized by these nine marks of health:

1 Expositional Preaching
2 Biblical Theology
3 A Biblical Understanding of the Gospel
4 A Biblical Understanding of Conversion
5 A Biblical Understanding of Evangelism
6 Biblical Church Membership
7 Biblical Church Discipline
8 Biblical Discipleship
9 Biblical Church Leadership

Find more titles at

www.9Marks.org

GOD

IS HE OUT THERE?

MEZ McCONNELL

SERIES EDITED BY MEZ McCONNELL

ISBN 978-1-5271-0296-5

IX **9Marks** | First Steps Series

WAR

WHY DID LIFE JUST GET HARDER?

MEZ McCONNELL
SERIES EDITED BY MEZ McCONNELL

ISBN 978-1-5271-0297-2

IX | 9Marks | First Steps Series

VOICES

WHO AM I LISTENING TO?

ANDY PRIME

SERIES EDITED BY MEZ McCONNELL

ISBN 978-1-5271-0298-9